Free
yourself
from Fear

Free yourself from Fear

Dr Lucy Atcheson

HAY HOUSE

Australia • Canada • Hong Kong
South Africa • United Kingdom • United States

First published and distributed in the United Kingdom by:
Hay House UK Ltd, 292B Kensal Rd, London W10 5BE.
Tel.: (44) 20 8962 1230; Fax: (44) 20 8962 1239.
www.hayhouse.co.uk

Published and distributed in the United States of America by:
Hay House, Inc., PO Box 5100, Carlsbad, CA 92018-5100.
Tel.: (1) 760 431 7695 or (800) 654 5126;
Fax: (1) 760 431 6948 or (800) 650 5115.
www.hayhouse.com

Published and distributed in Australia by:
Hay House Australia Ltd, 18/36 Ralph St, Alexandria NSW 2015.
Tel.: (61) 2 9669 4299; Fax: (61) 2 9669 4144.
www.hayhouse.com.au

Published and distributed in the Republic of South Africa by:
Hay House SA (Pty), Ltd, PO Box 990, Witkoppen 2068.
Tel./Fax: (27) 11 467 8904.
www.hayhouse.co.za

Published and distributed in India by:
Hay House Publishers India, Muskaan Complex,
Plot No.3, B-2, Vasant Kunj, New Delhi – 110 070.
Tel.: (91) 11 41761620; Fax: (91) 11 41761630.
www.hayhouse.co.in

Distributed in Canada by:
Raincoast, 9050 Shaughnessy St, Vancouver, BC V6P 6E5.
Tel.: (1) 604 323 7100; Fax: (1) 604 323 2600

All rights r⟨ ⟩ mechanical,
photograph⟨ ⟩ ⟨ ⟩ic recording;
nor may it ⟨ ⟩ be copied
for public ⟨ ⟩ embodied
in articl⟨ ⟩ublisher.

The autho⟨ ⟩ibe the use
of any t⟨ ⟩roblems
without the ⟨ ⟩ntent of the
author is on⟨ ⟩ your quest
for em⟨ ⟩ of the
informati⟨ ⟩ right, the
auth⟨ ⟩tions.

A catalogue record for this book is available from the British Library.

ISBN 978-1-4019-1581-0

Printed and bound in Great Britain by TJ International, Padstow, Cornwall.

C O N T E N T S

For all of us who have ever struggled with fears
and insecurities

ACKNOWLEDGEMENTS

I would like to thank all those involved in the publication of this work.

To Sarah Tay, with whom I wrote this book; the experience was lovely.

To Michelle Pilley for her belief in me and my therapy, and to all those at Hay House.

To Robert Kirby and Sophie Laurimore for their enthusiastic and tireless efforts.

And finally to my family and friends, who are so lovely and kind, and who help me in every way.

CHAPTER 1

INTRODUCTION

Your breathing is rapid. Your heart is throbbing. Your eyes dart around. Your palms are damp and clammy. Your arms and legs feel jittery. You twitch as if you're about to run a race. Your chest is pulsing. Your face flushes. Your palms squelch as you clench your fists. You're burning up. Your heart beats faster. Your jaw tightens. Your mouth dries. You feel detached from your surrounding, you feel almost lost. You have no control. You are in the grip of fear.

Fear is an emotion we can all relate to. It has always been part of the human make-up and it always will be, and because of this we all experience fleeting moments of fear within our daily lives. For example, we may feel worried about an interview; we might lose sleep over our child's exam results; we could be scared that our partner will leave us; or we may feel anxious about a medical appointment.

Fear spans a spectrum of intensity from insecurity to terror and, although it is at the milder end of the continuum, insecurity is the most common manifestation of fear. It is a human characteristic and affects every single one of us, so in this book I cover this form of fear first.

As you work through this book you will see that moving along this continuum from insecurity you will find, among others, worry, anxiety, phobias, panic attacks and post traumatic stress disorder. With so many forms of fear playing such a powerful role in our lives, do we have to sit back and accept it – or can we stand up to it? Can we fight back and overcome fear and insecurities that have been holding us back for a long time?

I believe we can fight fear in all its forms. I believe *you* can fight it – and that's why I have written this book. I want to show you that fear doesn't have to rule your life. I want to help you free yourself from any frightening emotions that you no longer want. But before I go any further, I just want to mention three things.

First, fear will always exist. There's no point me claiming that we can eliminate all fear from our lives, because we can't. No matter how much we learn to control our emotional state, there will always be things – both significant and less so – that will make us want to turn on our heels and run for our lives. But while you can't magic away all the things that frighten you, I can help you deal with them. I can show you about the various forms of fear, and share with you the techniques that will help you feel safe and in control so that you can teach yourself to beat them.

The second thing I want to mention is that, in dealing with fear, you face a classic Catch-22 situation. Fear makes you feel vulnerable and weak – but to beat it you have to be strong: you have to challenge your fear even when you feel like hiding. I know you won't always believe it and I'm not promising that this will always be easy – but I will keep reminding you that you can and will free yourself from fear.

The final thing that may surprise you is that by reading this book you may uncover things that you weren't expecting to find. While it may not make sense to you now, one reason why you may have found it hard to overcome fear in the past is because you hold a vested interest in being scared: an unconscious reason why you don't want to move on. You may be thinking, *What on earth do I get out of being scared?* – but many of us benefit from our fear.

Let me give you some examples. I worked with a woman who found it hard to overcome her phobia of paperclips because it kept her in a weak, vulnerable and child-like state so she didn't have to see the world as it really was. Another client found it more comfortable to invest all his mental energy worrying about spiders than to think about what else he would do if he didn't have to be constantly on the lookout for eight-legged creatures: he was more scared by the prospect of having mental freedom than he was by the thought of being liberated from his phobia. So while it may not be immediately clear to you, by reading this book you will discover whether the thought of changing unsettles you and whether, at some deep level, you don't really *want* to be free of your fear.

By the time you get to the end of this book you will have a deep understanding of fear and insecurity, and will be able to programme your brain to deal with these effectively. As you're reading this Introduction you may not even be aware of your fears and insecurities because you're so used to them, but they may be stopping you from having a healthy relationship, from getting the job you want or from fulfilling your dreams. Through the process of working through this book you will discover and confront your limitations so you can live the life you truly desire and deserve.

To get to this point there will be times when I will need to get hard on your emotions, but always remember that I'm not being hard on *you*. In this book I'm bringing my therapy out of the consulting room direct to you; to do this effectively I need to treat you as I would any of my clients. To get a successful outcome I need to be firm with your symptoms (and, as you'll see later in the book, this means being firm with your internal critical voice) but I will always be sympathetic with you. So when it might seem as if I'm putting my foot down, I'm only doing so because this is what's necessary for you to be able to break your patterns of behaviour.

If you're prepared to follow the techniques and tips I suggest, your fears and insecurities will no longer dictate what you can or can't do or how you feel. I will teach you how, even in the scariest moment, you can look your fear in the eye and say, *No way! I am not going to let you take control. I'm in charge!* By understanding fear more, you will be able to calm yourself down, take control and enjoy life. You will be the one in charge. You will have a different outlook on life *and* a different experience of life. You will be able to do whatever you wish – and life will be better than you could ever imagine.

HOW TO GET THE MOST FROM THIS BOOK

Read it all the way through

Because fears are often found together, I suggest you read the book from cover to cover. Even if you don't suffer from a particular condition, by learning about each fear you will see how they fit together and how one type of fear can grow into another. Plus, by understanding and appreciating other people's fears you will gain a general understanding of your own and others' behaviour.

Learn from the case studies

I find that, in addition to explanation, the clearest way to help people understand fear is to give detailed case studies of real examples. This puts theory into reality and will hopefully help you realize that other people share your experiences.

Note: Confidentiality Statement

At this point I would like to thank all of my clients, as working with them has enriched my understanding of psychology and human behaviour. While it is important in a book like this to illustrate such learning with case studies, I have taken every possible step to protect confidentiality. All names and other identifying features, such as gender, age, relationship status and profession have been changed; indeed, all of the case studies in this book present composite clients and are not based on particular individuals. The case studies here are typical of many clients and situations, therefore they may resonate with many people, but they are always representative of the many and never one particular case.

Take time to work through the recovery process

While there are some key themes running through each treatment process, each one is suited to a particular fear or condition. You will be able to pick out these exercises because they're clearly marked with this sign: Ω. I have taken great care to explain each process in a step-by-step format and, where possible, have related it back to a case study so you see the theory in practice. You may find that it helps to work with someone you trust – you will notice that for some conditions this is essential.

Be honest and fair with yourself

Apart from a few exercises where you need to work with someone else, many of the tips and techniques are things you can do on your own, so be honest about what you're feeling and keep remembering that this will all be worth it. If you've made the effort to buy this book and even to get this far into it, you owe it to yourself to be honest.

There may be times when the ideas and processes seem overwhelming but, as you will see as you work your way through, one concept that pops up time and time again is that *we tend to imagine things to be worse than they really are*. So if you feel scared at any point, take a deep breath, centre yourself and keep going. You can be confident that by the time you get to the end of this book you can feel totally different about how you feel about yourself and you can be free of your fear.

Take action straight away

Although the recovery processes take time to work through, in order that you can get to work on your fear as soon as possible, each chapter ends with some 'Take-home tips'. These are things that you can do *now* and they form the first steps to freeing yourself from your fear.

And finally…

You, the reader, are the person who is beating your fear, so give yourself credit every step of the way. As you understand more about your fear; when you engage with your rational thinking; for the times you take control of your internal critical voice; and as you eventually beat your fear – praise yourself. Celebrate the triumphs – and the small steps. In facing your fear you are being brave – and that deserves validation. Enjoy the journey!

WHAT IS FEAR?

Fear is the feeling of being intimidated *or* of being made to feel insecure about a situation, emotion or object. It is a personal thing: what scares one person may not feature on someone else's radar. There are people who are so terrified of open spaces that they won't leave their houses; and others who are so petrified of their own potential that they spend their whole lives feeling despondent and defeated. Some people feel scared at the thought of catching the train to work; others quake at having to organize a dinner party; and some people are so afraid of bananas that they can't even look at them. Fears like these are avoidable to a certain extent, although once you are scared of something it is surprising how frequently it appears in your life.

Whatever the form of fear, it's not the actual event, situation or object that is the real problem: it's how we *perceive* it. Take the example of someone who's about to do a parachute jump: while it may seem like a risky thing to do, believe it or not it's not the actual act of leaning out of the plane and stepping into the sky that causes the fear. What makes someone panic and shake and lose sleep for weeks on end is the thought of what *might* happen. *What happens if my parachute doesn't open? What if I break my legs when I land? What if a bird flies into my cord? What if I look stupid? What if I get up there and can't even bring myself to jump? What will other people think of me? What if? What if? What if?* So the first step in understanding fear is to accept that all fears come about because of concern about what may happen as a result of the event and *not* the event itself.

WHAT CAUSES FEAR?

If the object of your fear – for example, spiders, buttons, dogs or tall buildings – is not the cause, then what is? There are three main causes of fear: fear of other people's perceptions, fear of physical harm, and a fear of reaching our potential. I'll give a brief overview of each type of fear here and then you'll see examples of these through the case studies in each chapter.

I Fear of other people's perceptions

Most of us worry about what other people think of us, whether it's our family, friends, colleagues or even strangers, and we are familiar with thoughts like *What will they say if I wear that? What will they think if I do that? What will they do if I say that?* You may think it's a weakness to be concerned about other people, but everyone is a little insecure: it makes us human. It isn't healthy, however, for this fear of being judged to stop us leading our life as we would like to.

2 Fear of physical harm

This is the concern that we won't be able to cope with whatever it is we're going to do and that we will be harmed or hurt as a result. This could be about something as potentially dangerous as white-water rafting or something as routine as crossing the road. The threat of physical damage can be enough to debilitate us and make us avoid certain situations as an act of self-preservation.

3 Fear of reaching our potential

A lot of people believe that the greatest cause of fear is the prospect of failure; but while this does play a certain role, the fear of success plays, perhaps surprisingly, an equal part. There is also an existential fear of freedom and absolute independence: these two worries connect through the thought that if we try to reach our potential, we may actually be successful and our success would give us a whole new dimension of freedom that we wouldn't be able to deal with. People whose fears stem from this cause are scared that if they were to become too independent, they'd have to look at their life and see it for what it really is. Perhaps they'd no longer be locked in their limitations: they would have choices and so would have to deal with the possibility of life – and for many of us there is nothing more terrifying.

This is also related to the fear of maturing and coping on your own. It's the fear of not being able to cope with independence, making it seem safer to be dependent and to be looked after by others. As you will see, this is one of the reasons people develop phobias.

This type of fear is often harder for people to come to terms with because it seems less 'logical' than the other two types; one of the simplest ways to explain it is by saying, 'It's better never to try and never know how great you can be than it is to try, potentially succeed and ultimately fail.'

Almost every fear, regardless of its severity, stems from the belief that you are not able to cope – and so raises the same questions: *Will I be able to handle this? Will I be harmed? Will this affect me? Will it destroy me? Will I look stupid? What will other people think of me? Will I fail?* To overcome your fear, it's essential that you realize that your fear is based on an illusion: you can see beyond it and you can learn to cope. Empower yourself because you are, just as all of us are, capable of freeing yourself from fear.

HOW DOES FEAR AFFECT OUR EVERYDAY LIVES?

Fear manifests itself both physically and emotionally, to varying degrees. Those of us who experience a manageable amount of fear will be familiar with some of the symptoms, but in this book I will be covering several forms of clinical fear such as anxiety and phobias, so I want to clarify the difference between the feeling of passing fear and a continuous sense of terror.

Imagine you've been ill in bed for a few days and you're feeling tired and vulnerable. When you venture out of the house for the first time, you feel weak and a bit shaky. You're hypersensitive to everything around you – people, cars, noises, smells – and it feels as if someone has turned up the volume and brightness controls on the world: it's all a bit overwhelming. You go to cross the road and you're more vigilant than usual because you don't trust yourself and the world in general and you don't feel as if you can cope. You might feel like this for a day or so until you find your feet again. This is something that we can all relate to because we've all been ill at some point – but we know that these feelings pass. For someone who suffers from a mild phobia or form of anxiety, these feelings *never* pass: they feel like this all of the time. As you will see in this book, those who have acute forms of fear can suffer even more debilitating symptoms.

THE PHYSICAL MANIFESTATION OF FEAR

Most people have heard of the fight-or-flight response. This is the state we get into when we feel afraid and our body prepares us for two potential outcomes – face the situation and fight (literally or metaphorically) or turn and run. This heightened sense of danger makes our brain's messaging system work overtime. Our synapses fire much faster than usual from neuron to neuron because our brain believes we have something to fear and this makes our body pump out more adrenaline. This response triggers a pattern of reactions in the body. We may feel shaky and nauseous. We react to the slightest shift or sound, which can make our movements quicker and more panicked in nature. We can experience shooting pains and pins and needles in our arms. We may become teary. Our vision can be blurred and we find ourselves able to hear every tiny sound. Our senses are literally being bombarded with information, much of which the brain would normally filter out, and we become extra-vigilant. We become hypersensitive to what's happening around us because we process any piece of information that could threaten us – and so our environment can feel extremely overwhelming.

When faced with real danger the fight-or-flight response is a good thing, as we need a kick of adrenaline to help us run away or defend ourselves from whatever's attacking us; but when we're scared of things, situations and thoughts that don't pose a genuine threat to our safety and which don't actually require a physical response, these symptoms can lead to a vicious cycle of physical fear. For example, your initial fear response may cause you to move your head around nervously, to walk too fast with your shoulders hunched, to breathe in a quick and shallow way and to tense your muscles. This then leads to more adrenaline accumulating in the bloodstream without being released, so your body thinks there really is an imminent danger. This increases your fear response, which leads to more adrenaline being released, and so the cycle continues – this is how fear can feed fear.

CONFIDENTIALITY STATEMENT

Before I give my first case study I would like to thank again all of my clients, as working with them has enriched my understanding of psychology and human behaviour. While it is important in a book like this to illustrate such learning with case studies, I have taken every possible step to protect confidentiality. All names and other identifying features, such as gender, age, relationship status and profession have been changed; indeed, all of the case studies in this book present composite clients and are not based on any one individual. The case studies here are typical of many clients and situations, therefore they may resonate with many people but they are always representative of the many and never one particular case.

Case Study

I worked with a man called Peter who lived in London and had a phobia of getting on the tube. Peter was so afraid that he'd never actually got on a tube train, so it would be more accurate to say that Peter had a phobia of what he *thought* it would be like. His brain told him that tube trains were dangerous; he then generalized this fear to include tube stations and even tube signs: if he saw anything that symbolized tube trains he would experience the same fear reaction as if he were standing next to a train. As you can appreciate, this was a real problem.

Whenever Peter walked past a tube station his hands would sweat and his heart rate would rise to the point where, even though he was a young fit man, he felt as if he'd done a serious workout in the gym. His breathing became short and shallow. His shoulders hunched. His head would swim and he would feel like he was going to pass out.

Peter's fear was not about the physical act of travelling on the tube: it was about the loss of control that he associated with getting on the tube. He didn't have time to work out why or even if tubes were dangerous. He just felt the same physical reactions of fear every time he approached a tube station or sign. Because the physical manifestation was so strong it overwhelmed him and he never had the chance to deal with his fear mentally and rationally. To overcome his fear, Peter first of all had to learn to control the physical manifestations and slow them down.

Through our work together, Peter learned to control his breathing. This sounds very easy to anyone who doesn't suffer from anxiety, panic attacks or phobias, but when you're experiencing fear as intense as this, the seemingly simple act of breathing slowly can become complex and challenging.

To give him something tangible to do, I showed Peter the Hand Clasp Technique, which quite simply means putting your hand over your mouth, counting each inhalation and exhalation for three counts and forcing yourself to breathe through your nose. Nasal breathing is always slower and more calming than gasping through the mouth but again, as straightforward as it seems, when Peter was in the throes of a panic reaction it was difficult for him to think calmly enough to put his hand over his mouth and count his breaths.

Controlling breathing is essential, as it gives the brain a completely different message. It tells the brain that everything is OK, and this in turn initiates a whole new set of physical symptoms in the body: the heart rate slows, the muscles relax and the body comes back to a state of balance and control. When you're in this more relaxed state you can, as Peter was able to do, begin to investigate the cause of your fear.

If you want to overcome a fear, it's critical that you calm down the physical effects of fear in a controlled way. Throughout this book I will run through techniques that will help you control your body. Once you have managed to master your physical state, you will be able to analyse the psychological reasons for your fear and eventually overcome it.

THE MENTAL MANIFESTATION OF FEAR

The physical effects of fear are incredibly intense, but one of the reasons fear is so overwhelming is that the physical response is coupled with a less tangible but equally powerful mental response. The underlying emotion here is a lack of trust in yourself. When you are very afraid, you doubt your ability to function and cope; this self-doubt can be incredibly destructive to your psyche. Because you don't think you can deal with things, you not only feel negative about yourself and lose all hope about the future but you can also grow to fear your environment. This can really limit how you live your life.

These mental manifestations of fear may also lead to a sense of frustration because you don't *want* to be scared; you don't *want* to be frozen by fear. You may even be embarrassed by your fear and can see that, if left untreated, it could affect your future career, relationship, your security, friendships or your chance to have a happy family life. I would like to reassure you at this point that you have nothing to be embarrassed about. Fear is a human emotion, common to everyone in varying degrees.

You might also be aware that, if you had the tools to do so, you could overcome your fear – but if you feel you know this yet still aren't doing anything about your fear, this will chip away further at your self-esteem. You may wrongly feel like less of a person. This is where the cycle of disempowering behaviour can kick in.

When faced with your fear, you may tell yourself, *I can't do it. I'll never get this right. I'm useless. There's no point having a go. I'm going to fail.* You see nothing but threat and danger ahead, and may take it as a given that you won't succeed. With this kind of thought process running in your mind, your fear not only takes away your chance of being rational but also extinguishes any glimmer of hope, positivity and happiness in your life.

Case Study

Bridget was afraid of interviews and public speaking. She would go out of her way to avoid these situations. A couple of months before coming to see me she had had one particularly damaging experience: Bridget had had an interview for a job she desperately wanted. It was an exciting job a couple of grades above her current role and it involved more travel and responsibility.

In the weeks running up to the interview, Bridget managed to wind herself up so tightly that when the day arrived, she couldn't face it. She faked a migraine and missed the interview. Then, rather than rearrange it, she withdrew her application altogether. Because of the body's innate fear response, the options open to Bridget were to fight or flee;

and like most people who can't control their fear, she fled. But Bridget was not only fleeing one potentially uncomfortable and challenging interview – she was running away from the chance of a better future.

In the weeks following the missed interview Bridget obsessed about what she'd done. Instead of saying, *I don't care*, forgetting about it and moving on, every day Bridget would beat herself up for not going. She felt she had lost the battle with her fear. She saw herself as a loser, and although this was not true at all, she was convinced of it. Luckily for her, Bridget eventually realized that she had to overcome her fear. She could see that if she didn't, her whole life would be swallowed up by it and she'd never by truly happy. That was when she came to me for help.

We talked about how Bridget had built up the interview in her mind. Rather than simply seeing it for what it was – an hour of questioning and conversing – she saw it as a threatening situation that she couldn't cope with and something that could harm her. Her mind worked overtime thinking of all the possible negative outcomes. *The interviewers will think I'm inept. I won't get the job. I'll feel like a failure. Everyone will think I'm stupid. I'll ruin my reputation. I'll have to leave my job.* And so her thoughts kept spiralling downwards in a negative pattern until Bridget believed that by going to the interview everyone would think badly of her and she would end up thinking badly of herself. She could not see any positive outcomes at all and convinced herself from the outset that she was going to fail.

The reality was that Bridget had a very good chance of getting the job. Her CV was glowing, her work record was flawless and her reputation was excellent. But the reality didn't matter: Bridged doubted her ability so much that she couldn't trust herself to act normally in the interview. She thought she'd start laughing, that she wouldn't answer the questions and even that she would pass out.

In our sessions, Bridget and I worked out what the potential job actually meant to her. After several hours of assessment we found out that because of the travel involved in the new role, Bridget had equated this with more independence from her partner. This in turn revealed some serious cracks in her relationship, and it transpired that what she really feared was not the interview or even the new job but her future with her husband.

Bridget's husband didn't really pose a threat to her: he was just different. He was more introverted than her and didn't like to take any risks at all – from where they went on holiday to how they spent their weekends to the way in which they decorated their house. He was very traditional and conventional and Bridget wasn't. So Bridget, who had a relatively strong character, felt she had to compromise her own personality and needs to fit with him, and she felt that the new job would have meant throwing her relationship out of balance and could have led her to leave her husband. Bridget was trying to disable herself socially to become aligned with her husband's personality and mindset. This unconscious vested interest in keeping the status quo unconsciously maintained her fear.

Through our therapy sessions Bridget learned to compromise with her husband and she helped herself learn to care less about what other people thought about her by working out what she thought about herself. As a result, she had less need to fear public speaking and interviews, and she realized that she had the support of her partner.

WHY DO WE NEED FEAR AND INSECURITY?

When it can have such negative impact on our lives it can be hard to imagine that there is any benefit to feeling fear – but there is.

Imagine a world where everyone allowed themselves to run riot and do whatever they liked: where nobody thought about the consequences of their actions and everybody did exactly as they wished. We'd be living in a place where there was little in the way of a moral code or legal system, we'd have no social order and none of us would have any concept of responsibility. Partly because of fear, we do not live in a disordered world like this.

Fear and, to a certain degree, insecurity act as governing bodies in our society: they keep us in check and ensure we act with a degree of restraint. They help us realize our limitations and conform to society's rules. This conformity guarantees that the world stays relatively stable – both on a micro and macro level.

On a micro, or personal, level, our fears and insecurities save us from harming ourselves. For example, if we were fearless we would think nothing of jumping off a cliff or running in front of a car, both of which would be suicidal acts. This fear-induced self-preservation mechanism is particularly evident in new mothers, who experience a heightened awareness of the need to protect their children.

Fear also has the positive impact of improving performance. For example, one of my clients who was a very competent skier recently found herself on top of a piste and gripped by the fear of skiing down. She was completely convinced she would slip, but because she had no choice but to go down the slope, she took advantage of the surge of adrenaline to fight her fear: she directed her adrenaline rush to help her be more vigilant and ski more adeptly. Many sportspeople use fear in a similar way to intensify their performance: they find that they can run faster, throw further and compete more skilfully when, rather than allow themselves to be frozen by fear, they use it to energize them.

In most cases fear also gives us a moral conscience and helps us keep a check on our actions. But you only have to watch the news to see reports of murders, attacks and crises worldwide to see what happens when people act in fearless ways.

On a macro, or societal, scale, our fears and insecurities help to separate us into groups and so the natural order of society is created. On an even grander scale, if we look at fear from an evolutionary perspective, if humanity had evolved to be fearless, humans would have taken risks that would have jeopardized the future of our race and we would have ended up as an endangered species.

Fear is fundamental to life. It's not always negative. It helps keep us safe and guides us to take responsibility for ourselves. It enhances performance and governs society –

but for all the good it does, unfortunately there is a flipside to fear – and that's why I've written this book.

If you're extremely fearful of your limitations, then rather than fear making up a part of who you are, it becomes your whole identity. It can stop you from being the best you can be. It can get in the way of you living your life as you want to – and it can even stop you from living at all. I want this book to offer you a complete process for understanding, respecting and freeing yourself from fear.

WHY IS IT IMPORTANT TO CONTROL AND CURE FEAR?

Fear alters the way we see reality. Rather than see the world as a wonderful place full of opportunities, excitement and fun, fear causes us to see the world in a destructive way. We perceive it as dark or a place where danger looms at every corner – and for some people who have very extreme fears, this can literally be every corner. For some people a general sense of anxiety may mean that they have to steel themselves to cope with the slightest thing. For others their fear can restrict them to a very limiting routine and comfort zone – and this is no way to live. Regardless of the severity or type of fear you experience, this powerful emotion makes the world a smaller, less welcoming and seemingly more dangerous place.

Many people get caught up in their fear, which means they can't deal with the cause of it: rather than strive to overcome their issue, their main aim is to live life as best they can with their fear continually lurking in the background. Another way that fear limits our existence is that it forces us to act as if we're weaker, more immature and less able than we really are – and so it stops us becoming the best we can be. Fear simply makes us survive – but we can never truly thrive. The world can be full of amazing experiences, but none of us can enjoy what the world has to offer if we have to drag around a ball and chain of terror.

This is probably an appropriate time to acknowledge that some aspects of life *are* potentially dangerous. The world does unfortunately have some frightening elements, but these things are often not as dangerous as we decide they are. It's not the object of our fear that makes us scared – for example, a speeding car, barking dog or annual dental check-up – but our perception of it. We determine how scary something is through our perceptions and how much we allow it to threaten us. It sounds trite but, as you will soon discover, more often than not there really is nothing to fear but fear itself.

As you can see, fear can be totally devastating to life. Sometimes what starts out as a mild worry can, if left untreated, grow into a clinical form of fear – like anxiety or panic attacks or phobias. But you don't have to put up with it. There are *ways of thinking* that can help you cure your fears. I realize that this may sound strange, but fear exists in people's minds – not in their arms or legs. Fear stems from cognitive thinking; it is our response to objects and situations that causes, develops and maintains our fear. Fear is not an entity or a disease that you can catch; it is simply a way of seeing the world. So if you can change the way you think, you can change the way you feel, and free yourself of your fear. Some people go through their whole lives never facing their fears, but you have the opportunity to overcome yours.

HOW DO YOU FREE YOURSELF FROM FEAR?

In this book I will explain each type of fear separately, so within each chapter I will take you through the specific process for each condition; however, although the techniques differ, the underlying recovery process is based on the same key principles.

Understand your fear

I am going to try and show you how to gain control of your fearful thoughts by understanding them. When you understand your fear, you will no longer see it as either external to you *or* as an integral part of your personality. Whatever your level of the fear, you will realize that you can make a difference.

Face your fear

Be it a fear of giving presentations, of paperclips or of leaving the house, you can overcome it – and you do this by looking your fear straight in the eye. Because you will know how to calm yourself, you will be able to act rationally and get specific about your behaviour. I will show you how to speak to yourself in constructive ways. By stepping back from your fear, you will realize it's not as bad as you think. You only have to do this once to begin to build a new belief about your fear.

Change your behaviour

To cure your fear, you have to get control of your fight-or-flight response. You will learn how to slow down your reactions and define what you're really feeling, and this will help you get rid of all the other physical symptoms. You will no longer automatically fly away from your fear but will be able to face it in a calm way. You won't see your fear as a threat to your safety but as something you're going to get over.

Regain your self-belief

Once you can face your fear and address your thought processes, you will change the way you see yourself and the world around you. Whether you have a fear of flying or a fear of being abandoned, a big part of combating the physical and mental manifestations of fear is learning how to feel good about yourself. Then, no matter what gets thrown at you, you can cope with the panic, the ups, the downs and even the failures. You will no longer run away: and when you've faced your fear for the first time, you will have indisputable evidence that you *can* do it. This will prove to you that you can trust yourself, and so you will continue to overcome your fear. Hopefully, soon it will be a thing of the past.

CHAPTER 3

FEAR AND INSECURITY OF THE SELF

We all have insecurities about ourselves, and everything in our lives is affected by them: our internal dialogue; the way we project ourselves; how we perceive other people's lives; how we perceive ourselves; the way we see society; how much we enjoy life. Most waking moments are affected by our insecurities.

Insecurity is a form of fear – a fear about the self; and although the symptoms are sometimes milder than those of 'conventional' types of fear, I think that insecurity can be more debilitating and have a greater impact on the quality of our lives. For example, if you're afraid of spiders, when you see a spider your fear will be acute and intense but it will pass once the spider is gone. With insecurity, however, the experience is chronic, continuous and relentless, so the cumulative effect is greater. Insecurity follows you around and can do more damage to the soul – that's why I want to start by tackling this issue with you.

The types of insecurity I will cover are: fear of not being good enough; the expectation to be perfect; fear of failure;

fear of success; insecurity about image; insecurity about sexual attractiveness and performance; and insecurity of sexuality. These insecurities, if left untreated, can sometimes lead to much more serious and acute stress disorders, like social anxiety, chronically low self-esteem, eating disorders, body dysmorphia, addictions to physical-enhancement treatments, self-harm, identity crises, phobias, panic attacks, anxiety and agoraphobia. If any of these develops, insecurity becomes a chronic *and* acute disorder and has a truly profound and painful impact on your life and your health.

We can't just write off insecurity as being part of human nature: we need to manage it.

The underlying concern with all types of insecurity is that there is something wrong with you. All you have to do is turn on the television, pick up a magazine or newspaper or eavesdrop on a conversation on the bus to realize that most people, to some degree, don't feel comfortable in their own skin.

Case Study

Roger came to see me because he believed he was a fraud and an intrinsically bad person. He used negative words and phrases to describe himself, like *bad, harsh, embarrassing, unlovable, not good enough, pathetic and not masculine enough* – but he was totally unaware that he did this. When I asked him to give me evidence that he was any of the things he described, he couldn't find any.

This level of self-awareness was new to Roger because he had never asked himself why he didn't like himself or why he feared the fact that he was a fake: he had feared the answers so much that he had avoided the questions. What we unveiled during our session was that there was no specific event or belief that had led to Roger feeling false: it was as if he had a big, jumbled, confused mass behind him. He knew it was there because he could feel it following him around – and this dark mass turned out to be Roger's perception of his personality.

I helped Roger to control his fear response so that he could turn and face his personality as he had never done before. When he did so, Roger realized that there was no dark mass. There was nothing – and so there was nothing to be afraid of. It took time to get Roger to this stage, because anyone with such a deep fear of the self won't look at themselves because they're petrified of what they might find. So, in the same way that a phobic has to face their phobia, someone who is afraid of themselves has to stand and face who they are in order to realize they have nothing to fear.

Insecurity is rife in our society so I want to make sure you have the chance to explore not only what these issues are and how they manifest in our lives but also how to treat them. Hopefully, by the end of this chapter you will have taken the first steps towards freeing yourself from your fear and dealing with your issues of self-esteem.

FEAR OF NOT BEING GOOD ENOUGH

To a greater or lesser extent, we are all insecure and worried about how we present ourselves. We think about what we've said or not said, what we've done or not done, how good we look, how well we fit in and how popular we are. It may be hard to believe, but it's true. So if you've ever sat at a dinner table worrying about whether you're holding your own, chances are everyone else is more worried about the way they're performing than how you're doing. It is a shame, as we could all worry less if we realized that everybody does this.

This fear is all about judgement: you judge yourself according to how you think people see you, and appraise yourself according to the standards that you think other people set. *Was what I did good enough? How did I present myself? Did I say the right thing?* This behaviour pattern can be exhausting, particularly as it can affect every area of your life.

Have you ever come home from work and replayed your day, going through everything you said and did and analysing how you performed? *How did I do? Did I come across OK? What did they think of me? Did I make the right decision?* With all these questions running in your head, you probably worked out what you did well and cringed at what you perceived as not doing well.

You may also do this with social events. After an evening out, many people completely analyse their performance, from how many times they got a laugh to the number of times they said something they think was silly; the pauses in the conversation when they didn't know what to say; and the points where they felt they put their foot in it. They spend almost as much time going back over the evening with a fine-toothed comb than they did on actually enjoying themselves! The sad irony is that they probably don't need to do this self-analysis and are perfectly good enough as they are.

The fear of not being good enough is characterized by this need to over-analyse, but most of the time you face a losing battle because you cannot be objective about yourself. You're more likely to find things that went wrong than things that went right. In fact, in my experience the ratio of the perception of 'things done badly' to 'things done well' is usually 4:1 – that's four times as many things to feel bad about as things to feel proud of. In reality it's probably the other way around.

Case Study

One of my clients, Imogen, was high up in a blue-chip company and every day she would get home from work and, rather than relaxing, play back in her mind every meeting and conversation from the day to assess how she'd done. She would do this while she was on the way home from work, while she was cooking her dinner, while she was eating her dinner and also when she was getting ready for bed: that was almost three hours every night. It's not surprising that Imogen suffered from mild insomnia because she never let her mind be quiet. She also used to comfort-eat to try and distract herself from her thoughts, but this only made her feel worse.

Given how stressful her job was, what Imogen really needed to do when she got home was switch off, but she never allowed herself to. She would highlight all the things she thought she'd messed up. For example, if she was going over a new project plan in a meeting, she'd worry that the ideas she'd put forward were no good and that she hadn't given enough attention or credit to someone else's ideas that were actually better than hers. To rectify what she'd done, Imogen would write down what she would say to her colleague the next day. She would check with them that they weren't offended by her initial dismissal of their ideas and she'd do everything she could to make them feel better.

The next evening, after she'd had that conversation, Imogen would spend an hour or so replaying it to make sure she'd said the right thing and that she'd made her colleague feel secure. She'd then worry that she'd made too big a thing out of it, but knew she couldn't go back to them to check, as she would have lost her all her professional respect and reputation. But rather than leave it and move on, Imogen would worry about the conversation and go back over it again and again, torturing herself that she'd messed it up.

As you're reading this, you're probably realizing how exhausting Imogen's thought processes were. You can see how tiring and draining it was for her to invest all her mental energy in analysing every little thing. One hour-long meeting would lead to up to 14 hours of appraisal, follow-up and analysis. Imogen also spent days planning for meetings – even longer than most people, because she felt she had to be meticulous in her planning to avoid messing up. She could spend up to six hours working out what to say and how to act with each person, so that one meeting could lead to a total of 20 hours of mental investment. Imogen was naturally astute and intuitive, but she never trusted her intuition – she felt more comfortable analysing. This ritual was taking up her time and energy and causing her to feel terrible about herself. It's no wonder Imogen was shattered!

This pattern also appeared in Imogen's social life. If she'd been out with friends, when she woke up the following morning, especially if she'd had a few drinks, she would write down whatever worries she had about the night before. For example, if she was worried that she'd been insensitive, she'd jot down all the bits of evidence she could find that she had been. She'd then rate each thing she'd done or said to someone on a scale of 1 to 10; if it was higher than a 4, she'd ring up that person to check they'd got home OK or to see if they'd had a good time. What she really wanted to know, though, was whether they were still talking to her or whether she had insulted them beyond repair.

This constant self-monitoring was a symptom of the fact that Imogen had very little self-confidence. She couldn't believe that what she did and how she acted was good enough, so she picked holes in everything and had pieces of evidence from every single day to prove that she was inadequate – and with this evidence Imogen fed and nurtured her insecurity.

This fear of not being good enough is created in our own minds. We see failure where others don't. We see inadequacy where everyone else sees ability, and we find fault where there is none. We also create our own strategies to cope with our insecurities, but ironically it is through these coping mechanisms that we give ourselves evidence to prove that our insecurities are real. By analysing and judging ourselves we inevitably find more fault. Although we don't mean to, we end up colluding with our fear – just as Imogen did.

THE EXPECTATION OF PERFECTION

Chasing perfection is an endless and futile task. You feel as though everyone expects you to be perfect, but this expectation is inherently problematic because none of us is flawless. You can do a job well, you can be very handsome or pretty, or you can have a great personality – but you can never be perfect. You can be slim or funny or a fantastic cook, but it's impossible to say you are flawless and that you can never get any better. The goal posts will always keep shifting, because every time you do something and *almost* get it right, you know you can do better. You never allow yourself to reach your goal and so end up beating yourself up that you haven't done well enough. By setting unattainable standards you always let yourself down – and this erodes your self-esteem.

The other element of this expectation is the need to compare yourself to other people – but this is also pointless. There will always be someone whom you perceive to be more organized, smarter, richer, funnier or more attractive than you, so because in your eyes you're never the best, you will never feel good enough.

Case Study

Geoff wanted to be perfect all the time: the perfect husband, the perfect father, the perfect friend and the perfect employee. He was actually pretty good at everything he did, but nothing was ever good enough for him. If his work was all in hand, Geoff would then worry that his CDs were out of order and he'd give himself a hard time. If something was out of place on his desk, he'd think, *I'm such a bad manager; I let things get out of place,* and he'd take everything off his desk and tidy it up. His insecurity was so great that it encompassed everything he did – so he'd have to take control over entire tasks to make himself feel better.

Geoff was constantly telling himself he wasn't perfect and that he had to criticize himself. Not only did his imperfection cover all areas of his life, but so did his criticism: he'd start by picking up on the fact that there was a bit of mud on the floor of his car and this would become an obsession that he was a failure. He would drive himself mad with wanting to be perfect and ended up suffering from anxiety. What started out as a quest for perfection and a motivation to do everything well became self-bullying. Geoff almost destroyed himself in the process.

It's very common to generalize and catastrophize your insecurity in this way. With this insecurity everything becomes 'all or nothing': you're either completely perfect or absolutely terrible; nothing is ever in between. But ironically, almost everything we do in life is 'in between'. It certainly was in Geoff's case.

What's so sad about this drive to be perfect is that people who suffer from it are always good enough just as they are; in fact they're often above average in most things they do – they just don't realize it. If they could see this in themselves, they could avoid suffering from anxiety and fear. But they just can't see this.

As with all insecurities and fears, there is no reality-based evidence to prove this type of insecurity is true. They are founded on **F**alse **E**xpectation **A**ppearing **R**eal. There is no proof that you're not good enough. In the case of chasing perfection, the expectation to be perfect is in itself false – it only seems real. Perfection is unnecessary and so is the turmoil suffered in pursuit of it.

I want to take this opportunity to say that this insecurity can lead to minor rituals and over-fussiness about being neat, which can sometimes then lead to obsessive-compulsive disorder and other psychological disorders. If you suffer from this, you don't have to learn to live with it. You honestly can deal with it before it takes over your life.

THE FEAR OF FAILURE

If you're afraid of failing, you see the threat of failure at every turn. Because you think failure is terrible, you're scared by the thought of it and your fear makes you notice every opportunity where you could fall down. You can't just be getting ready to go out: you have to get ready to go out on time and look really good – otherwise you will have failed. You can't just be cooking a meal: you have to cook a delicious meal – otherwise you will have failed. You can't just be collecting your children from school: you have to pick them up on time with a healthy snack to hand and you have to be looking presentable – or this too will be a sign that you have failed.

Like most insecurities, if you fear failure you see failure where it doesn't exist and daily life seems to be a series of tasks and tests. Everything in life becomes a chance to succeed or fail – nothing simply *is*. The ironic thing is that even if you do succeed, the fact you're so worried about failing means that you'll think you've failed anyway – so you just can't win. If you get 97 per cent on an exam, you'll wonder why you didn't get 100 per cent. If you pass your driving test, you'll see your success as a failure because you were a bit wobbly on one of your manoeuvres. Even if you can't find anything you did wrong, you'll write it off as a fluke: you can never let the evidence that you've succeeded speak for itself.

All insecurities are a filter through which we see the world. If you see the possibility to fail all around you, you become so convinced you're going to fail it becomes a self-fulfilling prophecy. You'll find a way to fail, no matter what.

Case Study

George was afraid of failing at work. He'd never actually failed at anything in his job and was very good at it, but he told himself that it was only a matter of time before he slipped up. Rather like Imogen, he'd get home and replay his day and analyse it until he found all the tiny things he could have done better. George was so set on looking for evidence to back up his belief that he always found it: but the things he was picking up on were things that most people would just let go. Most of these were things that he himself hadn't even noticed at first because they were so tiny; but because he would scrutinize everything he did, he would eventually find mistakes. They weren't critical errors and other people didn't notice them, but George would beat himself up that he'd failed. He'd then rush into work the next day and tell someone what he'd done; even though his colleagues weren't usually bothered, George was determined to make a big thing of it.

He would then torture himself by looking for reasons why it mattered. Rather than say, *That wasn't a big deal*, he'd say, *Well, it was a big deal and next time it will be an even bigger deal*, and so he'd carry on searching for proof that he was a failure.

If you look for evidence hard enough, just as Imogen, Geoff and George did, you'll find it. If you think your partner's cheating on you and go through their phone you will find a text that has a tiny ambiguity in it that you could read as a sign of infidelity. Even if your partner is not cheating, if you're hell-bent on believing they are, you'll be able to turn whatever you find into proof that they are having an affair. Basically, if you're looking for evidence to prove something you believe, whatever it is, you'll create the evidence and it will appear real to you.

Sadly you won't realize what you're doing until you step back from your behaviour and stop thinking in terms of black and white. Try to reframe how you see things and look at 'failures' for what they really are. Rather than divide life up into failing or succeeding, everything you do is a shade of grey and it doesn't matter if you get the odd thing wrong.

Everything in life is 'in between' or a shade of grey. It's not a case of failing or succeeding or of being perfect: things just are the way they are and you don't have to be afraid of them.

THE FEAR OF SUCCESS

Fear of failure is a commonly accepted fear and many people will acknowledge having it to some degree; but another insecurity that is also common, much more common than you may think, is the fear of success.

The negative outcomes of this insecurity come about through the life choices you make because of your fear. You never give yourself the chance to shine because you always make sure you don't stand out from the crowd, and you never let yourself feel the flush of pleasure or the rush of adrenaline that comes from achieving something. You tend to avoid putting yourself first; you avoid taking credit for things you've done; you avoid trying to do well, whether in your professional or your personal life, in case you do actually succeed; and you don't collect evidence that you're a good person. Instead, the evidence you collect builds up a picture that you're not as capable or as successful as you really are.

Case Study

Jessica was the youngest of three children and the product of pushy parents. They weren't pathologically pushy but she saw the hard time her parents gave to her older siblings to make sure they did well both academically and in extra-curricular activities. As the youngest, in order to avoid being lectured by her parents on why she should do better, Jessica simply didn't try. Jessica was afraid that if she succeeded at something, everyone would then expect her to do well at *everything* and that one success would lead to a lifetime of having to live up to everyone else's expectations. So Jessica didn't allow herself to do well at anything and her parents never realized she could achieve: they just let her scrape by.

Jessica's coping mechanism to avoid being pushed led her, in her teenage years, to not pushing herself. This then 'generalized' (spread to affect more areas of life) in adulthood to become a fear that, once she was successful at anything, other people would expect her to be successful all the time. Because of what she'd seen her parents do when she was younger, she thought that her boss and even her friends would expect her to keep up a top performance and she'd never be able to live up to it. Consequently Jessica only ever had mediocre jobs and, if she did do anything well at work, she let other people take the credit.

This fear of success also affected Jessica's personal life. When she did choose to be with someone, she made sure they had no expectations of her. Because of her fear she'd never had any confidence in herself, and when she met her first serious boyfriend he took advantage of her; inevitably, after years of being mediocre and playing second fiddle to everyone else, Jessica also started to take herself for granted. She saw herself as a 'grey' person and not as likeable, distinctive or with anything to say for herself or show for her life. What had started out as a strategy for getting herself some space as a child, ended up as a strategy that was totally diminishing her self-esteem.

This fear of success is linked to the fear of trying hard, the fear of being positive about yourself and the fear of complimenting yourself. All of these have the effect of lowering your self-esteem and, moreover, these fears can exaggerate each other. If you never push yourself to do anything different, you never have to stand out from the crowd. By knowing that you've never tried to do anything different or achieve anything, you begin to believe you're not capable. Eventually your self-esteem becomes so low that you don't think you're good at anything. Then when you realize that you might want to have a go at doing something, your fear stops you from trying. You see yourself as an indistinct personality and force yourself to live an average existence. This leads you eventually to believing that you're dull and worthless.

If you feel this way and experience this negative cycle of behaviour, you need to break this pattern before it goes any further. It may seem as if you've felt this way your whole life, but you *can* change and you can do so whenever you choose – just have some faith in yourself. Even if this is hard, it is possible.

INSECURITY ABOUT IMAGE

This kind of insecurity is common to everyone. We all *care* about how we look. We all *think* about how we look. We all *worry* about how we look. There are countless diets available to (supposedly) make us look better. There are problem pages dedicated to image. Many television shows are about how to look more stylish, younger or simply more attractive. People talk about looks all the time – it's a more popular topic of conversation than the weather! *You're looking great. Ooh – she's lost weight. Aren't you looking well? I love your outfit* and so on.

Let's be realistic for a moment. We know we're judged on how we look and, whether we'd care to admit it or not, we also judge other people on how they look. As hard as it may be to accept, most of us do judge others on appearances. Take a common example. Say you pop out in your tracksuit and happen to pass a smart shop. You go in but the shop assistants don't give you much time or attention. Some may even look you up and down with disdain because you don't look like you can afford to be in there. But if you go back when you're dressed up, the assistants fall over you because they'll make the assumption, based on how you're dressed, that you have money.

This kind of judgement is a part of life and, as much as we may not like it, it's widespread. But when it's taken a step too far – when you're preoccupied and obsessed with image and an incessant insecurity about how you look that prevents you from doing what you want to do – that's when it becomes unhealthy. Not going out for the evening because you don't have a posh enough dress. Not going on a date because you don't believe you look good enough. Not going to the gym because you feel too fat. Not leaving the house because you're having a bad-hair day. All of these things are examples of how image insecurity can be taken one step too far and really depress us.

This kind of obsession can, if left to grow, lead to an eating disorder like anorexia or bulimia. You can see from the recent hot debate about size-zero models that this is a very real issue. Some women are so obsessed about getting down to a size zero that they'll chew on paper, smoke non-stop to kill their appetite or even stop eating altogether – and in some very tragic cases, some women have died in the pursuit of thinness. Other people turn to surgery to make themselves look perfect; I'm sure you can all think of people who've been under the knife several times in the endless pursuit of 'perfection'.

In theory there is nothing wrong with wanting to make the best of yourself. The decision, for example, to have surgery, comes down to individual choice and can be made both from a positive and a negative standpoint. If you think you look good but that you could look better with a bit of enhancement, this is the positive stance: on the other hand, if you think you look awful and ugly and need to do something radical to your looks to become acceptable, that's the negative stance.

However, most people who are insecure about their image don't have a sufficiently realistic picture of themselves to make a rational choice as to whether or not to have surgery. If you see yourself in a distorted way, having surgery won't change that; even if you look different, you won't *feel* different. For example, if you can't see anything positive about the way you look and think you're too ugly to leave the house, having surgery won't suddenly make you see yourself in a positive and realistic way. If you are only able to see yourself in a harsh and critical light, going under the knife won't change that.

One of my clients had very successfully lost weight but, when she looked in the mirror, she still saw herself as fat. She couldn't accept that she was responsible for making the best of herself and she assumed her fat must be hiding somewhere. She wanted surgery to shed even more weight, but my concern was not that she wanted the surgery (that was her individual choice) but that if she couldn't see the positive effects of her weight loss efforts so far, she wouldn't be able to appreciate the results of surgery either. If after the surgery she still gave herself a hard time and saw herself as an overweight person, it would all have been for nothing. If there was no positive effect of surgery, she was in danger of falling into the trap of having more and more surgery to 'improve' herself without ever being happy with the results.

You have to think you're good enough as you are. If you do, then you can take healthy steps to improve yourself. If you don't, you need to work on your insecurity first and then think about enhancement.

Case Study

Wendy was really disappointed with her image. She stopped herself from getting in touch with friends from her previous job because she believed she could only do this when she had the perfect life: swanky car, dream house, gorgeous man, huge salary, a big-shot promotion at work and a size-10 body. She was holding herself back from going to reunions and would always find a reason why she couldn't: she had too much work, was too tired or had family commitments. But the real reason holding her back was that she didn't think she had the right image to face her old friends.

Wendy was determined not to see them again until she had achieved everything on her wish list, but all this did was put her under even more pressure. Her enjoyment of life in the present moment was not what it could have been because she wasn't letting herself see the people she really liked. Of course her friends didn't care about her image and would just have liked to see her to catch up – but to Wendy, her image was the be-all and end-all. The real shame was that Wendy was a truly lovely person just as she was.

Obviously it is not just women who are insecure about their image: men are becoming increasingly self-conscious about how they look.

Case Study

Dave was an ex-personal trainer and he left this job to work for a fitness company designing fitness products and programmes. Inevitably, after leaving an active job and becoming desk-bound he gained a bit of weight, but he wouldn't go back to his old gym to train until he looked as good as he used to. Dave couldn't bear people seeing him not as he was when he used to be so fit, but by keeping himself away from the gym he wasn't able to use the training equipment he needed to look the way he used to. Dave just couldn't see that his gym buddies would want to see him because he was fun to be around and a genuinely nice bloke – all he focused on was his few excess pounds.

Both of these case studies show how over-concern about image can lead you to forget about your personality – in fact, it can make you forget about the very essence of who you are. All you do is focus on what you *don't* have; as a result you reach a point where you no longer like anything about yourself. What starts out as insecurity about your image can end up as genuinely low self-esteem – and this is created in three ways: through your thoughts, your feelings and your behaviour.

You have thoughts like: *I have to wear better clothes. I need to be thinner. I should be more successful. I wish I drove a better car. I have to have a perfect relationship*. Your feelings focus on emotions like embarrassment and dislike for yourself, and through your behaviour you avoid people and tell yourself you're not good enough to see them. These things chip away at your self-esteem and so you believe that by not having the right car, partner, body or lifestyle other people will reject you – but they won't. What actually happens is you end up rejecting yourself – and that's why insecurity about image can be so devastating. You begin by worrying about wearing the right clothes or dropping ten pounds, but by focusing on your weaknesses and ignoring your strengths you end up disconnecting from your authentic self.

INSECURITY OF SEX AND SEXUALITY

As with image, thinking about sex takes up a lot of our mental, emotional and physical energy – and almost everybody thinks about it. *Am I getting enough? What is the national average? Is everyone having more sex than me? Am I good in bed? What does my relationship say about me? Do I satisfy my partner?*

Ironically, when we analyse our sex lives – rather than going with the flow of the natural instinct of two bodies being together and enjoying each other – sex becomes a judged task which takes away all the satisfaction. If you're always thinking about how well you're doing, how much you're enjoying yourself or how much the other person is enjoying themselves, sex loses its point – it's not meant to be a cerebral activity!

Case Study

Lucas was very insecure about his sexual performance. When he was in bed with a woman he was so convinced he was doing a bad job that he would spend the whole time inside his head questioning whether he was doing the right thing and whether the woman was enjoying herself. So the intuitive natural element of sex was lost: it became sex-by-numbers, which meant that there was no excitement or intimacy. Lucas ruined the act for himself and for whomever he was with – and this in turn added to his insecurity.

This fear can also extend to sexuality. *Am I gay? Should I be straight? Is it OK to be bisexual? Am I the right sexuality?* Whatever your concern, if you're worried about your sexuality you are judging something that is innate, something you were born with, and this chips away at the very fibre of your being. You are born gay or straight and you can't do anything about whom you're attracted to. You are who you are, and being insecure won't make you have better sex. It will make you worry about it, and this will ruin your relationship and your life. Sexuality is not a disorder that needs fixing and so there is no need to be insecure about it.

Case Study

Joseph thought he might be gay; when he first came to me he had been in denial for a few years. Although nowadays both marriage and children are possible for gay people, for Joseph being gay meant not having children and not being married. He was worrying so much about his sexuality that he wasn't letting himself get on with his relationship and enjoy it. He had met a man whom he was seeing in secret and he couldn't accept that he should just be with him and acknowledge him as the person that he loved.

Joseph got very insecure about who he was and couldn't accept it. He refused to be seen in public with his partner and it was only when his partner threatened to leave that Joseph realized what he felt and who he was. Joseph realized that he had to do something about his insecurity or else he was going to lose the man he loved and who loved him. While they did manage to work through it, Joseph's insecurity was needless and nearly threatened the happy, healthy future of his relationship.

Whether it's the way you look or the way you talk; whether you're afraid of failing or of being successful; whether you're worried about your sexual prowess or your communication skills – all of these insecurities come down to one fear: the fear of not being good enough. The belief that in some way you're not good enough causes you to stop being who you really are because you believe you have to be somebody different.

But where does the difference lie between the real self and the ideal self? If you're so wrapped up in coping with your insecurity, would you even notice if you became the ideal model you'd set out to be? Are you really striving to be a better person or are you condemning yourself to a life of insecurity? While you have this vision of the Ideal Self, you'll never allow yourself to enjoy life and be who you are.

Ω *Overcoming Insecurity*

The answer to getting over any kind of insecurity is to support yourself and play to your strengths. The process for doing this may seem very simple, but as with all of the treatments in this book, it only works if you follow it. This might sound a bit silly, but you'd be surprised how many people would read this and then turn the page and keep on reading without doing anything. If at any point you feel like doing this, stop and do the exercises. If you do them and follow the tips below, I promise that you'll thank me in the long run.

1 Compliment yourself

I want you to start by using compliments. It is possible to like yourself for who you are and realize that who you are is good enough. People worry that this will make them seem arrogant, but it won't, as it doesn't mean going around telling everyone else how amazing you are: it means saying to yourself the kinds of things you say to other people: things like *You look nice. You did really well. You're good at that. You're fun to be around. You're a great person.*

So it would be positive for you to list all the things about you that are positive – your strengths, the things you do well, your skills and talents and the things other people like about you. Then read this list every day.

Please don't worry. I'm not asking you to be over the top: I'm suggesting that you simply change the way you communicate with yourself, because liking yourself is the starting point for recovery.

I may remind you to do this many times throughout this book and you may even get sick of me saying it but I will repeat it because it's so important. *You have to like yourself to support yourself.* It's a critical element of overcoming every fear – whether it's a minor fear or insecurity or a serious phobia or anxiety disorder.

2 Look at who you really are

This next step is a reality check. On one piece of paper write down who you think you are at the moment, including how you look, what you do and what you have in your life. Then on a second piece write down who you'd really like to be, covering all the same areas.

Now that you have these two lists, read them and look at the differences between them. Try to quantify this gap. Is it as much as you think it is? Are there things about your Ideal You that you already do or have? Are there things about you that are good enough? Is the Ideal Self actually achievable – or is it an expectation that's simply too high? Have you created a super-human model that you can never become? Have you set yourself up for failure?

Case Study

Franklin came to me for treatment because he had a very negative self-image. When he did this exercise, this was what he wrote:

Actual Self	Ideal Self
Plain	Interesting
Conformist	Successful
Bit dull	Articulate
Unsuccessful	Free-thinking
Boring	Spontaneous
Passive	Assertive
Not living to potential	Good looking

When we looked back at his Actual Self list, I asked Franklin to give me a concrete example to prove each of the things on his list: he couldn't give me evidence of any of these negative traits. Then I asked him to give me examples of the characteristics on his Ideal Self list. After I gave him a gentle nudge, Franklin found all sorts of evidence! He was interested in the arts; he was very successful in his career; he had loads of friends who wanted to spend time with him; he had proved himself as being assertive in a recent confrontation at work; and so the list went on. He had proof of every single one of the traits on his Ideal Self list, he just hadn't been able to see this without stepping back from himself.

The process of realizing who you really are was termed self-actualization by Carl Rogers, and most people are much closer to becoming their Ideal Self than they realize. If you find that you're closer to your Ideal Self than you realized – even if you can only find evidence for half the things on your list of ideal qualities – acknowledge that part of you already is the way you want to be – and enjoy it! You need to enjoy the here and now and accept that you're good enough just as you are. Realize that you have a choice: you can continue to strive for a future that will always be out of reach – or you can value the present and enjoy the life you have now.

3 Create a strategy for change

If you do find through this process that there are things that you genuinely want to change, take a rational approach to tackling them.

1. List these changes and then, next to each one, write a strategy for how you're going to go about it.

2. If you can't devise a strategy, it's perhaps because the change is unrealistic. In this case you have to reject it as unnecessary and unachievable. Acknowledge this and focus on being happy with that part of you as it is now.

For example, one thing many people want to change is their weight. In following the above strategy process, avoid creating an extreme plan of action – for example, dropping two waist sizes in a month. Think about what you'd advise a friend to do and make sure the steps are realistic and achievable. This may be walking to and from the train station; cutting out your mid-morning packet of crisps; swapping ice cream for yoghurt.

Another common area of discontent is career: if you want to change your job, don't be rash and resign on a whim with no idea of how you're going to make ends meet. Make a step-by-step plan that will get you successfully to where you want to be. This may include seeing a careers advisor; getting work experience; talking to people about their jobs; studying a new subject; going part-time in your job so you can spend a day a week really investigating your options.

TAKE-HOME TIPS

1. Find three positive things to say about yourself. Say them out loud. Try it now!
2. When you go to bed tonight, just before you fall asleep, congratulate yourself for three things you did well today. There will be three things, as everything counts – no matter how small it might seem to you.
3. If you have been afraid to do something for a long time, write down one thing you can do in the next week to get the ball rolling. Support yourself by being kind to yourself and make sure you do it!

ONE FINAL THOUGHT ...

Most people will be striving for perfection because they think it will make them successful and more likeable, and that these things in turn will bring them happiness. Well, instead of taking the long route to happiness, why not take a short cut and be happy just as you are? All that's standing between you and the chance of being happy and secure in yourself is your perception of who you are. You don't have to change who you are: you just have to change how you see yourself.

CHAPTER 4

FEAR WITHIN RELATIONSHIPS

Culturally we are somewhat preoccupied by relationships: we write songs about them, films are mostly about love and when you meet a friend you either ask about their partner or, if they're single, the conversation turns at some point to whether they've found anyone yet. As a society we have a historical and cultural belief that we need a relationship to be happy, but I don't think we can make sweeping statements about love as some people thrive as part of a couple and others fare better when they're on their own. As individuals we need to do what makes us happy. But for those of you who are worried about your relationship – or lack of relationship – we're going to explore the kinds of fears and insecurities that are found within relationships and what you can do to overcome them.

Our relationships can make us feel fantastic – and they can also cause us a great deal of pain because we don't have as much control over them as we do in other areas of our life. For example, if you want to make sure that your career is going well you can study to get the right qualifications to work your way up the ladder. There may be some other factors to work around, such as bosses, bullies, supply and demand, and glass ceilings, but on the whole you have a great degree of control over your career. When it comes to your health, you can choose how active you are, what you put or don't put in your body, how much sleep you get and how hard you party: you prioritize your health. In relationships, however, we depend on another person to do their share to make the relationship work, and this can leave us feeling vulnerable.

The worries around relationships are endless. When you're single you worry about meeting someone. Then when you've met someone you worry about whether they're right for you and if you're right for them. Then you worry about how to take the relationship from the first flush of romance to a more serious level. This leads on to worries about commitment and moving in together. After that you get concerned about whether you're compatible enough to survive all the things life will throw at you: commitment, pregnancy, children, bereavement, house moves, job changes, sexual problems, middle-age crises, old age and all the other ups and downs to come. Do you feel like you're missing out by being together? Does your partner feel they're missing out? And so it goes on. Because of this long list of potential worries we can end up analysing every detail – and making ourselves very insecure in the process.

To help you have the best personal life you can, first of all I will write generally about fears arising from social comparison. Then I will take you through the most common worries about relationships to consider how to deal with them. They are: fear of not being good enough, fear of being with the wrong partner, fear of rejection, fear of change and fear of commitment. Hopefully, by sorting out these issues you will find it is easier to enjoy your present and future relationships.

FEARS ARISING FROM SOCIAL COMPARISONS

The need to compare yourself socially can affect anyone, so don't be too hard on yourself. Everyone worries when they're with someone that they might miss out on someone better. You might also be worried that everyone else if having better sex and/or more sex than you. You may be convinced that other people see shooting stars and fireworks every time they see their partner. You focus on the everyday elements of your relationship – the dirty socks, the tedious trips to the supermarket and the unromantic early nights – and, to some extent, assume that you're the only one whose life is like this.

When you're single, on the other hand, you may compare yourself by worrying that everyone is better than you and that you must be missing out on things. You think everyone is having a fantastic relationship and you don't know how to get one. You believe everybody has an amazing social life but you don't seem to be a part of it. Everyone is going on fabulous holidays but you don't know where to go. Everyone has a close-knit group of friends and you have only a few mates. It seems that everybody is incredibly confident apart from you. Nobody is as insecure as you and nobody is as lonely as you.

In all these cases, without really knowing what everyone's lives are truly like, your imagination exaggerates the difference between you and them – and, as I've said before, this kind of irrational thinking is often referred to as **F**alse **E**vidence **A**ppearing **R**eal. There is no way of proving that you are worse off than anyone else, so making comparisons will always make you feel bad about yourself: you see other people's lives through rose-tinted glasses and you see your life warts and all.

THE FEAR OF NOT FEELING GOOD ENOUGH

We are tribal beings and our evolutionary history dictates that it's natural for us to want to be around other people; so we are born afraid of loneliness and none of us truly feels comfortable with the idea of being on our own. So if you do find yourself alone, you may become very defensive and, as with many fears in this book, you can grow to accept what you see as your fate and live as though you really will never meet somebody until it becomes a self-fulfilling prophecy.

The thought that you're single purely through random circumstances can be hard to deal with, so you may also tell yourself that it's because there's something wrong with you. Although this is more painful, we tend to be happier with the idea of having some degree of responsibility and control over our destiny. It's easier to say, *It's me – and not society – that is at fault,* but this is something that has to change. You have to tell yourself that you are good enough to meet somebody and that you will meet somebody. Try to give off this message of confidence through the thing you really can control: your behaviour.

Ω *Act As If You're Good Enough*

When you go out you need to send messages to other people that you are good enough through the way you walk and the way you move.

This technique takes 5 minutes and I suggest you do this every time you're about to go out – and especially before any kind of social event.

1. Stand in front of a mirror and drop your shoulders. This makes you look strong and assertive without being overpowering. Put your hands by your sides and keep your feet flat on the floor. Tell yourself that you're grounded. Feel grounded and strong and keep your head and eyes level.

2. When you feel ready, find ten compliments to give yourself. This may be uncomfortable or even painful at first, but everyone can find ten things. If you struggle with this, ask yourself what other people might see in you – then, even if you don't agree, say these ten things out loud to yourself.

3. Next, close your eyes and think about something or someone you love or like or have recently enjoyed. It could be your mum, your dog, your best friend, a slice of chocolate cake, your football team, a great night out or a funny joke. When you get a warm feeling from that thought, open your eyes and look at yourself with that feeling still in your mind – then leave the house.

This may seem like a simple or even a silly thing to do but, believe it or not, by seeing positive things about you and by projecting a feeling of warmth onto yourself you start to turn your negative self-image on its head: it all started in your mind, so you can break it down by changing your mind. The fear that you might not meet anyone is caused by not being in the right mental, emotional and physical space – but this exercise puts you in the right space. Even if you've been thinking that there aren't enough good available women or men to go around or that you basically aren't good enough, this exercise starts to tell your mind that you are good enough and that you can – and will – meet somebody. If you're still hurting over a past relationship, by seeing the positive in yourself you will grow stronger and so will be more able to see clearly when you are ready. If you're worried that life is unfair and there are no decent single people left, by feeling good about yourself you can see that there must be – and when you like yourself more, you also feel less alone.

THE FEAR OF BEING WITH THE WRONG PARTNER

Another common fear in relationships arises when you are actually with someone but you don't think they're right for you, and so you analyse your relationship: rather than focusing on it being about the two of you, you see the relationship as being between two people and their pasts; two people and their ideals; two people and their friends; two people and their insecurities; two people and their goals. By bringing into the equation all these other elements, you make yourself afraid that you're not with the right person – and this isn't purely based on them as a person but on how they fit with all the other factors in your life. You might also focus on your partner not being right for you as a protection mechanism in case you do split up, because if you didn't think you were good together in the first place you can't get hurt if the relationship ends.

Whatever the reason, if you're afraid you're with the wrong person, you can convince yourself that everything's wrong and end up ruining the relationship anyway. This is because you are probably intellectualizing your relationship – but relationships are fundamentally emotional, so it's better to acknowledge how you feel, not what you think.

Ω Let Your Emotions Rule

Our emotions make us human. Many of us think that emotions cloud our judgement and that we have to think rationally: rather than accept a feeling of love, you may wonder if you're talking yourself into loving your partner; or rather than go with the feeling in your gut that says someone is right for you, you look for evidence that they're not.

You may also become disassociated from your emotions because you don't stop to feel them. When was the last time you asked yourself how you felt about something? Most of the time we rely on what we *think* and ignore what we *feel*, as if we're scared of listening to our emotions.

So, instead of letting your fears flood you – let your feelings flood you. Make the time and space to acknowledge your emotions and pay attention to what your body is saying.

Your body is very clever and will tell you when you're doing the right thing – so watch out for the good signs – flutters of excitement, a sense of relaxation and contentment and a desire to smile! – and the not-so-good – dread in your stomach, headaches and persistent tiredness. While everybody feels their emotions differently, deep down we all know when something is right and when it isn't; you just have to be brave enough to accept the signals. Then, once you've done this, you need to be sure what those signs are saying.

Ω *Look Behind Your Fear*

Fear is one of the most confusing human emotions. Because of its intensity, what many of us do is ignore it and hope it will go away. As you will see for other areas of fear, however, to overcome your fear you have to roll up your sleeves, take a deep breath and get to the root of the issue.

Sometimes it's really hard to see clearly what your fears are. The way to work out whether you're just over-analysing and picking holes in your partner because you're scared of being left or whether there really is something wrong with your relationship, you need to look behind the fear.

Case Study

As Nita got close to her boyfriend, she began to believe he was going to leave her and that she wouldn't get the happy fairy-tale ending she really wanted out of life. To deal with this, because her partner had to travel a lot for work, Nita made an issue out of the travel. She started to question whether she could bear to be in a relationship that was, for much of the time, a long-distance one. She couldn't stand the idea that, if they got married and had children, during the week she would effectively be a single mother. Nita wondered if it really could work and whether her partner would choose his career over her, and so she talked herself into leaving him.

Looking at this retrospectively during the therapy process, the travel hadn't actually been an issue for Nita when she was with her partner. She'd enjoyed having time to herself to go to the gym, catch up with her girlfriends and generally have space to think and do her own thing. When they were together, the fact her partner was away most of the time during the week meant that at weekends they made a real effort to go out and do lovely things together. In fact, Nita had been so unconcerned by him being away that she'd never even brought up in conversation whether he would change job for her.

She never knew the truth but she had created the answer in her head: that he would never leave his job for her. Nita's obsession that her boyfriend would leave her became a reality and she ended up heart- broken. Nita then even managed to reframe the circumstances in which they'd broken up by twisting reality in her head so that she remembered it as him leaving her because he thought his work was more important.

Ω *Work Out What You're Scared of*

To get to the real issue you need to stand back from your situation and take a rational stance. The best way to do this is to structure your thoughts by writing them down.

Take a piece of paper and divide it into three columns.

In the first column, write down all your fears and insecurities about your relationship.

In the second column ask yourself, *Does this fear relate to me – or does it relate to my partner?*

Be honest! In the final column, answer this question: *Does this really matter?*

Sometimes you can work out your fear on your own, but in some cases you'll need to talk to your partner. Many people have no idea what their partner feels about them, or even how they feel about their partner, because they never ask. You have to make the time to discuss your feelings and be open with each other because, as you can see in Nita's story, when you try to *guess* what someone is thinking, you usually imagine the worst-case scenario. It's better to know the real picture so you can deal with it.

Two-way communication

You have to talk. It doesn't have to be a heavy conversation about having children and being together for ever, but you should have this kind of conversation when you both have time and space and when you're relaxed. Don't be tempted to raise issues when you've just had an argument – as we all know, this is unlikely to call forth a good response!

Ω *Get Talking*

When you find an appropriate time, focus the conversation on whether you and your partner are enjoying the relationship as it is now.

Are you having fun in the moment?

Are your feelings reciprocal?

Are you both heading in the same direction?

If your relationship is further along the line and you are thinking about commitment, then it's OK to talk about this too. It's better not to avoid the topic and make up your own answer because you'll end up wasting emotional energy worrying unnecessarily.

If your partner tells you how they feel about you and you choose not to believe them, then you need to accept that the issue lies inside you. It's probably an issue about being left and rejected: if you don't trust anybody to ever stay with you, you will probably force the relationship to end and so will have created a self-fulfilling prophecy.

FEAR OF REJECTION

It can be very hard to admit that we're afraid of being rejected. You may demand signs from your partner that they love you even if you're not sure you love them. You might find yourself wanting to get married or have children because you think this will tie you together. You might test your partner to see if they'll leave you. However this manifests, you probably never actually ask yourself what you want – but what you want is the most important question of all.

Ω *Put Your Needs First*

If this fear of rejection resonates with you, I want you to stop for a moment and ask yourself:

What do I want?

If you are afraid of rejection, you may answer something like:

Not to be alone
Not to be rejected
To be with someone.

Then you have to ask:

By constantly worrying that nobody wants me and telling myself I'm not good enough, am I rejecting myself?

It's useful to clarify whether by feeling you have to be with someone just so you don't have to be on your own, you are rejecting your own needs and wants. If you are only with your partner because you need to be part of a couple, you owe it to yourself to find happiness. Remember that what you imagine it will be like to be alone is usually worse than the reality. You can enjoy your own company and give yourself time to work out who you are and what you want, so that when you are ready to meet someone you have a greater chance of choosing a person who complements you and makes you happy.

Fear of change

Most of us are afraid of change, but not many of us are prepared to admit it – especially when it comes to our relationships. Many of us would feel embarrassed to admit that we were at first afraid of living with the person we love or of having a child with someone we've lived with and shared our lives with for several years. We think that to be exciting and interesting we have to take risks, but we're not all naturally inclined that way. There's nothing unhealthy about being scared of change – but it can be unhealthy to deny or ignore this.

Case Study

Maggie and Jack had been together for five happy years when they came to see me. They knew they were right for each and they had always been faithful. When I asked them how they saw their future, both of them could clearly imagine being together indefinitely and having children together. They both knew that life would be very different but they could still see themselves going through all those changes as a couple. If they thought about not being together they felt devastated, but Maggie and Jack couldn't make the connection between living together now and their future lives. So the problem wasn't in the future: it was in the present moment.

When they actually needed to make the first step and move in together, both of them, but particularly Jack, kept making excuses about why they shouldn't move in together. They blamed work and finances and other practical issues beyond their control as to why they couldn't change anything; but these were really rationalizations because they were afraid of change.

This is another example of **F**alse **E**xpectation **A**ppearing **R**eal. Maggie and Jack were afraid of what they thought change meant and the upheaval they assumed they'd have to deal with. They spent every night together and so didn't feel the need to combine space, and they liked being in control of their own space: they enjoyed having boundaries and they had no idea how they'd share that control when they were living together. They were intimidated by the thought of negotiating these boundaries and of compromising.

If you've been single or have dated for a long time, the thought of moving in with someone or of getting married can be petrifying by virtue of the fact that it's different. We all find routine soothing and secure, so the thought of making a big change, even if it's for the better, can scare us into inertia. Just as you might get nervous about changing jobs even if you hate your current job; or might stick to driving the same old car for years even when you can afford to buy a new one; or might resist changing your hairstyle because you're used to it, you can see that fear of change is all around us – and relationships are no different.

There's no point distracting yourself from the real issue, however uncomfortable it may seem: you have to tackle it head-on and face the facts. Acknowledge that life is going be different and talk about how you feel. Dare to put the truth out there and forget the pressure that many people feel to jump ahead without a care in the world.

Ω *Yes, but ... Analysis*

The first step in dealing with the fear of change is to clarify what the fear is really about. You have to see that it's not about money or promotions or dealing with family illness, or about waiting for a change in the property market – it's all about being afraid of the change itself.

To identify the fear and see it for what it is, here's what you need to do.

As a couple, take a paper and pen and write down every reason why you don't want to take the next step. How many 'yes, but…' excuses have you been hiding behind? Here are some examples:

Yes, but…
… we'll wait to see if I get a promotion
… the rental market will pick up
… we need to find an unfurnished flat so we can take our own things

... in three months we'll have more money to rent
... my job's unstable so I daren't move
... we're not sure where we want to live.

These are just some of the excuses you might have been using, but you also need to take time to work out your own. Then ask yourselves what this is really about and analyse each point. How long have you been using that reason as an excuse not to move on?

When you've worked out what is scaring you and you know you really want to be happy, you can deal with the real problem constructively.

Ω *Spot the Difference*

We can often feel vulnerable when we discuss our relationship because it's such an emotionally charged area. Here's a way that you can identify how you feel about change on your own.

Ask yourself how you feel about change in different areas of your life. When did you last embrace change? When did you last do something different – something momentously different? For example, changes in your career, hobbies, sports you play, friends you see, the car you drive, your health and exercise regime, your image or the clothes you wear.

When you have thought of these things, split them into two lists: one list of things you've enjoyed and felt comfortable with changing, and another of changes that you felt forced into making or changes that seemed really difficult or painful.

Next look at these lists and honestly ask yourself:

1. Are there more changes that happened because your life got out of control and you had no choice or because you wanted to make that change and you embraced it? How many changes were 'shoulds' and how many were 'wants'?

2. To what extent do you hide in your comfort zone – and to what extent do you actively seek out change?

3. Now work out your ratio of routine:change. If the ratio is significantly tipped in the favour of routine – if it's a ratio of 4:1 or higher – it's likely that you are living your life with an unconscious motivation not to change.

Fear of change is common, so there's no need to feel embarrassed or upset by it. The best thing you can do is acknowledge it and realize that while many other people live their lives afraid of doing things differently, you are one of the few who is going to take action and combat it – and the best way to do this is to change your thoughts.

You don't need to use mantras or write long lists, you just need to give this some attention and think about how your fear is holding you back. If you never do anything differently, won't you become bored with life? If you decide to do everything as you always have done, aren't you giving in to the existential fear of your own freedom?

We are all born with this existential fear, and you will see that it crops up many times in this book. This fear is like a very strict and overbearing parent who won't let us do things as we want to and won't let us spread our wings to see how far we can fly. Within the area of relationships, by not seeing how far you can go, you can end up limiting yourself and never finding out how amazing your relationship could be.

FEAR OF LONG-TERM COMMITMENT AND FAMILY LIFE

Getting married or committing through a civil partnership and having children are incredibly emotional steps in life. Although being in any relationship means being bound together, these stages require a greater level of emotional binding, and in many cases legal binding too. If you want to split up you face more difficulty because you either have to go through a lengthy and expensive legal process or, if you have children, you have to deal with never truly separating because you share the common bond and responsibility of your children.

For these reasons you can understand why people don't take these decisions lightly. I agree that people should not jump into this level of commitment without serious consideration – but at the same time if you avoid them completely you risk missing out on some of the most satisfying and emotionally rich times of your life.

Striking the right balance in this decision process between not taking it lightly and not being petrified is all about being clear on whether you and your partner love each other enough and whether this is what you truly want. We all know that successful relationships are hard work; you need to be sure that you're prepared to put in the time and effort needed for years to come. People change and circumstances change, so at every stage there are things that look after themselves and there are things that need attention.

When you first get together you usually can't keep your hands off each other and tend not to have to think about your sexual connection; but it's in those early days that you have to work at other things like getting used to each other's routine, friends and family. Then as these areas of companionship become easier, you usually have to work on the sexual aspect and this can be one of the most problematic areas of relationships because it's inherently contradictory.

The one place where people can acknowledge craving change is in their sex life, because the strongest desire humans have is for unfamiliar touch. So although fear of change may make you scared of leaving your partner, because you have physical cravings for something different you can find yourself enticed by the temptation to be unfaithful, thereby sabotaging your relationship. Alternatively you may find you don't want to commit because you think this rules out the chance of ever experiencing someone else's touch.

Although this situation may seem tricky it can be handled if you're aware of it. You need to find ways to maintain excitement and interest for both of you, because you don't actually need unfamiliar touch from another person: you can bring the unfamiliar into a stable, faithful relationship.

The commitment tests

It seems that we can put too much pressure on ourselves when it comes to commitment and we often turn it into too big a deal. Many of my clients say to me that they don't know if they're happy and ready to commit because they have no idea what that kind of happiness feels like. Although we may not be aware of it, we have a continual dialogue with ourselves about how content we are, so we *can* actually work out if we're happy and in love through the internal dialogue we run as an integral part of our daily lives.

Ω *Use Your Emotional Feedback System*

You run an emotional feedback system as part of your internal dialogue. Start by becoming aware of the things you ask yourself like: *Do I like this coffee? Am I enjoying my job? Do I look good in these shoes? Am I pleased with how this is going?* When you are comfortable asking yourself about little things like these, you can generalize this and ask yourself how you feel about bigger things: *Do I love my partner? Am I happy with where our relationship is going? Do I feel secure? Are we having fun together?* These questions are a natural progression from your daily internal chatter – you just need to make sure you're asking yourself these questions rather than being too afraid to confront the answers.

Ω *The Front Door Test*

Another way to ascertain whether you're happy in your relationship is through what I call the Front Door Test. You know you're happy when you open your front door and you'd rather your partner were at home than that they weren't. It's lovely to be as comfortable and at ease when your partner is by your side as you are when you're on your own.

Also, happiness is not all about feeling butterflies and seeing fireworks. You may feel excited about seeing your partner, but the main emotion you should look for is a sense of contentment and belief that all is right with the world when you're together.

Hopefully you can see that you're ready to commit to someone when you feel more complete and more like your true self when you're together than when you're apart.

You should look for reasons to be together and, if you are apart and you experience something really positive or negative, the first person you want to tell should be your partner. You know you're happy when you think life is more fun as a couple.

If you're not happy or ready to commit, however, you need to be honest about it. Maybe you don't trust your partner; or you have tears behind your eyes when you think about your future; or your partner puts you down and criticizes you; or you get anxious at the thought of seeing them; or routine tasks become chaotic and end in arguments and you don't know why. All of these things prove that you are unhappy in the relationship. As much as you may not want to admit it, if your relationship is defined by emotions and situations like these, you're not afraid of commitment – you just know that commitment is not right and it is time to leave. The status quo is not always the healthiest state for relationships: sometimes it's time to move on together and sometimes it's time to move on apart.

TAKE-HOME TIPS

It may take time to find the right person or to sort out your relationship, but there are some things you can do straight away to start the process of finding happiness:

1. If you are on your own and are afraid of not meeting anybody, write five compliments about yourself and repeat them in front of the mirror.
2. If you are dating someone but aren't sure if they're right for you, write a list of all the pros and cons of your relationship. Look at the list to see whether it's worth staying and enjoying what you have.
3. If you're dating but have a fear of commitment, make a list of pros and cons of your relationship to see whether you are happy. If you are happy and the only thing stopping you from moving on is your fear, make the decision to work on this through the processes in this chapter.
4. If you're scared of getting married or having children, write a list of why you're motivated to stay as you are. If the list is of things that are negatively motivated, for example, *So I don't lose my partner* or *Because I'm scared*

of being trapped, then you know what you have to work through. If your list is positively motivated, then you have nothing to fear: you are in the right space and can take the next step.

ONE FINAL THOUGHT ...

You will have seen in the last chapter on insecurities, and you will go on to see in several chapters in this book, that when it comes to fear, what we *perceive* is always worse than what's really out there. This is particularly common in relationships because we all want to be loved. To get over your insecurities and be open to love, you have to face reality because it's always better to deal with what you see and what you know, than to deal with what you imagine to be true.

CHAPTER 5

FEAR AND INSECURITY WITHIN THE FAMILY

Everyone can relate to this kind of insecurity, because to some degree we all struggle with our families. Our family members know us better than anyone else: they know our background, our history and all the things that we'd rather people didn't know. They tend to see a side of us that we hide from others; it's this that makes us vulnerable to their opinion.

The extent of this insecurity can vary depending on whether it's caused by daily family life – things like expectations, family scripts and guilt, all of which I'll explain in more detail later in this chapter – or by really destructive behaviour within a family, which leads to a more serious form of insecurity and which I will write about in more detail in Chapter 7. One thing I will say, however, is that insecurities and fears within families all grow from the same seed. It is caused by the way we are treated by the people who are supposed to protect and love us.

Case Study

Maria was a high-powered businesswoman. Within her working environment she was respected and she called the shots, but with her mother she was completely different: she couldn't say 'no.' If her mother rang up, Maria would drop whatever she was doing to attend to whatever her mother wanted. She never took time off when she wanted to. She spent every Christmas with her mother and always took her away on holiday with her family. She felt she had to include her mother in everything she did, and as result she had an unbalanced and strained family life. She was so afraid of being disapproved of that she altered her own actions and even her identity to make her mother happy.

I worked with Maria to make her realize that her fear of losing her mother's love was inappropriate. It was as if she believed she couldn't exist without her mother and that her identity was reliant on her mother's approval. This meant that even though she was a grown woman she could never separate from her mother and her mother still held all the power in their relationship. Maria had to learn to trust that her mother's love was solid and start to take back the power she projected onto her mother in order to be her own person.

What Maria experienced is, unfortunately, very common. Many people are scared of saying 'no,' so they manipulate their own identity to fit with their family's perceptions of them. They fulfil the role set for them by others, so they don't get to live life on their own terms. While it's admirable to want to make other people happy, it's not healthy to do so to your own detriment. You don't need to be selfish to have a sense of yourself; you just need to be comfortable with the idea of setting boundaries.

THE FAMILY CONTEXT

The family unit is a context for insecurity because, as we grow up, it is our most important developmental environment. From when we are babies through to our teenage years, much of our learning is done within the home or when we're around family members. It's understandable and even logical, then, that the family can have great influence over our self-esteem – and this starts very early on in life.

Because of our need from a young age for parental approval, parents are in a unique position in the process of human development. The very first way that any human starts to develop an awareness of their identity is around the age of two when we see how our main carer, usually our mother, looks at us. If we are looked at with love, we compute that we must be worth something – we must be special. Our parents' reaction means everything to us, so if we don't feel loved and protected by them, we assume it's our fault. It is because of this that parents can cause immense insecurity.

We also assume our parents are right, so if our parents do something wrong we don't see that it's their fault or issue – we blame ourselves. For example, if a couple get divorced, children often blame themselves. If parents smack their child, the child will think he did something to cause it. Even if parents abuse a child, the child will think that the abuse is his fault. Rather than thinking, *What's wrong with my parents?* the child thinks, *What's wrong with me? Why don't they love me?*

This parental power has immense hold over a child's psyche, and this power relationship can play out and lead to insecurities in several ways: following family scripts; creating a scapegoat; drug abuse or alcoholism; family expectations; and family-induced guilt – whether deliberate or accidental.

Family Scripts

Rather like being cast in a play, within a family people are often allocated a role and script – a character that fits with the rest of the family members. These roles come together to create what's called a family script. The kinds of roles you often see are: *She's the clever one. He's the sporty one. She's the kind one. He's the funny one. She's a handful. He's so naughty.* Each person plays their role and so the family story, or drama, unfolds.

But families are not the only environment in which we get typecast or labelled. Labelling happens among friends, for example: *He's the joker in the group. You can always rely on her to lend you money. He's the one who'll make sure we all get home safely. She always gets the most drunk.* It also happens in the workplace: *He's the organized one. She's the one who'll stay late. He's always the last in the office. She's always the one who messes up.* Whatever environment we're in we all put labels on others and we all get labelled ourselves – but labels can be very damaging.

As we grow and mature, our personalities change and so do our needs. When you're about five or six years old you desperately want to fit in with your family because you're human and humans don't like to stand out or be rejected. As you begin to get older and develop into a teenager, however, it's natural to feel the need to discover who you are. However, because of the labels you're given, you tend to get typecast all through your teens and adulthood. While in reality you might be funny one day and moody the next, or you might be naturally chatty but every now and again go through a quiet phase – more often than not during your moody phase or on your quiet days, your family either won't let you be that way or they'll think there's something wrong with you.

This can happen on a day-to-day basis and it can also happen over a longer time scale. For example, say you were not a sporty child but then after puberty you discovered your sporting ability and became very physically active; chances are you would still be labelled as someone who was 'not sporty' because that's how people think of you. Or maybe you were very shy in your teens but once you started working you became confident and so by your mid-twenties you'd become much more outgoing, your family would probably still call you The Shy One. Those who know you well do whatever they can to get you to stick to your role, because this is how they know you and this is what they feel comfortable with.

I don't know if you've ever tried to remove a sticker from a CD or a label from a beer bottle: You can pick away at it for ages but there's always a bit of the label that won't come unstuck. It's the same with character labels. Labels and scripts cause damage because they have a permanent feel to them even though what they're labelling is transient. They don't give room for development and they don't allow you to change and move on from qualities that may no longer serve you in your life.

Case Study

One of my clients, Nick, had been a mischievous child. He used to have a seriously naughty streak and was the exact opposite of his sister, Susan, who was a clever, obedient child. Susan won a scholarship to private school and her parents found her easy to manage – not like Nick. Nick was the one who bent the rules – the one who always got into trouble - and while Susan passed all her exams with flying colours, Nick only ever scraped through. Their parents came to expect them to play out these roles for ever – and for a while Nick did.

When he got into his teens Nick became caught up in recreational drugs. Despite having always expected him to be a bit wayward, this was a step too far for his parents because it didn't fit with their family script. They had very traditional values, so when Nick became involved in this scene his parents thought he'd gone off the rails and so devoted all their attention and efforts to Susan: in their eyes, rather than just being the cheeky one who had a mind of his own, Nick had become the black sheep.

Nick's parents couldn't see that this was a passing phase. He was only dabbling in drugs and he still managed to get through university and get a decent degree. Eventually, Nick got bored of parties and the drugs scene. He got a good professional job and started to do very well for himself. But despite all of this, Nick's family still saw him as the black sheep and Susan as the golden girl. However, both Nick's and Susan's lives continued to diverge from the roles that were expected of them.

Nick reached the top of the ladder in his profession and he was really getting on with his life. Susan, on the other hand, struggled to settle into a career. Her insecurity was made all the greater because her family had always expected her to jump straight into a fantastic job and excel at it; for once she was not playing out her role within the family script as expected.

Nick's and Susan's roles had been reversed. The labels their parents had stuck on them when they were children were no longer suitable, and this caused confusion and upset for everyone. Susan felt like she was letting everyone down because her parents had always assumed that she would be successful, while Nick felt the pressure of making it on his own because he'd never had the support of his family.

Nick felt that no matter how successful he became, it was never enough to change his label and win his parents' love and approval – and he was right. Susan buckled under the pressure of having to achieve to be loved. Although for very different reasons and because of very different family scripts, both Nick and Susan felt insecure.

Labels and scripts are dangerous because they cause comparisons, and whenever we feel we are unfairly compared, we become insecure. If you are given the positive script you can experience great pressure to achieve and may feel insecure that you will only be loved so long as you continue to do things well. If you start to struggle with life, as most of us do at some point, you get scared that your parents will no longer love you as they used to. If you are cast to play the troublesome role you can feel misunderstood and unsupported and can become afraid of being rejected – and that prospect terrifies most of us.

Because of the way evolution has panned out we are reliant on our parents for much longer than any other species, and so we are genetically programmed to be scared of their rejection. We are innately afraid that if our parents reject us, we will be left to fend for ourselves, so we often resist forming our own personality and identity. But our identity – who we are and how we act – is very fluid, particularly in our early years when we are changing and developing at a very fast rate; so whenever our identity is not allowed to change, naturally we can become insecure and afraid.

THE SCAPEGOAT

Labels and scripts are most damaging when they are used to turn someone into a scapegoat. When someone is scapegoated they are seen as being a 'bad' person or 'less of a person' than everybody else. This harmful comparison in turn leads to more unfair and unnecessary mistreatment. You may be picked on and emotionally abused and you may also be physically or sexually abused. Emotional and physical abuse often go hand in hand, though they can also be found separately. However, regardless of the nature of the abuse, the child victims are made to believe that they are the worst person in the world. Because of the way they are treated, they are likely to end up with the belief that the world is a terrifying place.

Case Study

Georgie was the third and last-born daughter in her family. After their first two girls her parents had really wanted a little boy and, while they didn't verbalize their disappointment, they showed a continual undercurrent of disappointment that they had had yet another girl. Georgie picked up on this disappointment and became an archetypal tomboy: she played sports with her father that were more typically played by boys, like football, and she dressed and acted in a boyish manner. This contrasted with her sisters, who were both very feminine. Georgie thought that by playing a different role her parents would be more likely to love her.

What actually happened was that because she stood out from her sisters, Georgie became the family scapegoat. None of her family members ever verbalized this, but if anything went wrong in the family Georgie sensed her parents' and sisters' rejection, and so she shouldered the guilt and blame. Just through her family's reaction to her, Georgie felt inferior and rejected.

The insecurities that stem from this fear are far-reaching and if they're not dealt with they can also be long-lasting. Unless you free yourself from the guilt and fear, you will never lose the belief that the world is completely unsafe – you are incapable of protecting yourself – but to do this, as I have said before, you have to realize that the abuse was not your fault. You *have* to believe and accept this to leave your negative emotions in the past.

SURVIVORS OF ALCOHOLICS AND DRUG ABUSERS

Insecurity can also stem from a family environment in which one or both parents or carers are drug addicts or alcoholics. If you grew up witnessing addictions like these it makes sense that you would create the belief that the world is unsafe and then carry that into your adulthood. Because of your contact with drug users or alcohol abusers as a child, you were not made to feel protected when you most needed it. If this environment is all you have known – if you have never had any evidence that you can be made to feel safe and loved – how are you to know any differently?

We all know at a fundamental level that the world isn't a safe place. Every time we turn on the television or read a paper we are bombarded with news of crimes, wars, shootings on street corners and rapes – and it seems as if there is no end of threats to our safety. But if you are secure in yourself you know that statistically these things are unlikely to happen to you and you are also probably fairly confident that you know how to protect yourself and avoid danger as far as is possible. You trust yourself and, if a threat were to come along, you believe at a deep level that you would survive it. You also take steps to keep yourself safe: you think, *If I avoid poorly-lit roads at night I'll be OK. If I keep my mobile phone hidden from view I won't get mugged* – and so you manage to rationalize your chances of being hurt.

If you have been brought up by a drug or alcohol addict, however, your view of danger and safety is somewhat skewed and so you also have slightly skewed strategies for keeping yourself safe. You generally feel more vulnerable and, because you exaggerate the chances of danger, you are likely to take exaggerated steps to counter this danger. You might think: *If I touch this light switch 50 times I'll be safe. If I stick to my routine, I'll be OK. If I keep everything clean, I won't be harmed. If I never go anywhere on my own, nothing will happen to me.* These coping mechanisms can be the start of obsessive compulsive disorder, which is another reason why this kind of insecurity should be dealt with as soon as possible.

I want you to understand that both kinds of strategies for keeping safe are similar: whether you avoid dark alleys or whether you wash your hands incessantly, you are doing these things because they make you feel secure. The underlying beliefs are the same and they are rational: it's the steps you take to control the world that can become irrational and extreme – so washing your hands won't make you immune from attack but you believe it will.

FAMILY EXPECTATIONS

Families can also cause insecurity unconsciously and without malice by setting expectations. Even though parents tend only to want the best for their children – because of the need to see their children do well and often because the parents think they know best what will make their children happy – they set expectations that, although well-meaning, can ironically lead to insecurity and a fear of being judged.

Case Study

Claire felt she never lived up to her parents' expectations. Her parents had been happily married since their early twenties and had had three children whom they expected to take similar paths – but Claire's personal life had taken a different route. At 34 she was about to leave her second husband and had not yet had children. She felt guilty that she was letting her parents down, but the reason she was soon to go through her second divorce was because she was actually desperate to try to find a man she thought her parents would approve of.

What Claire couldn't see was that her parents had approved of both her husbands and the real reason her marriages hadn't lasted was that the men she picked weren't right for her. Her family never judged her boyfriends or husbands and never told her what to do, but because she was so determined to please her family, Claire was choosing men through her parents' eyes and not through her own. If she had gone for *her* choice of man, she would actually have been able to enjoy the long-lasting marriage she thought she was expected to have.

As you can see, expectations don't have to be voiced or shown explicitly. They may never be openly expressed but if you don't *believe* you live up to your family's expectations, you will feel judged regardless. You may think, *Did I live up to my parents? Did I do as well as I could have done, given my background? Did I let my family down in any way?* If you look hard enough you can almost always find a way in which you let down your family.

Case Study

Ian had done very well for himself in the world of finance. He had made a lot of money and reached a level of success that made his parents immensely proud of him. Because he felt that he had achieved over and beyond what his family had, however, Ian felt that in some way they might think he was snubbing them or making them feel as if they hadn't done well enough for themselves. He had wealth far beyond what they had, a career that they had never achieved and he got to experience things that they could only dream of. While Ian gave his family a lot of support financially and shared many of his experiences with them, he still felt that he was rubbing their noses in his success. As a result he felt bad that he'd made his family members feel insecure about themselves. Even though they assured him that they felt nothing but pride and happiness, he believed he'd hurt them.

GUILT

The final way in which we can become afraid and insecure of our families is through guilt. Sometimes our family members mean to make us feel guilt and sometimes they don't; regardless of this, the family unit is the perfect environment for guilt to take root and grow.

Case Study

Veronica thought her mother expected her to go and stay every three weeks, and she also felt she had to attend every major family event and so curtailed her own life so that she could visit her parents regularly. This affected Veronica's relationship with her partner because he always had to fit in with her visits home. If they went on holiday Veronica would feel guilty and insecure that she was a bad daughter because she was leaving it longer than usual between visits. This guilt was ruining her relationship, her enjoyment of her visits home and even her hard-earned holidays. She was riddled with guilt and was at breaking point when she came to see me.

It transpired from Veronica's therapy sessions that she and her mother enjoyed a wonderful friendship and that in her early twenties they had been particularly close, as it was at that time that Veronica had really needed her mother. But as her mother got older and became more vulnerable, Veronica projected that her mother needed her as much as she had needed her mum all those years ago.

Her mother had never said this but Veronica had assumed it, and so thought she had to be the perfect daughter.

Veronica's drive to be perfect made her feel inadequate because, as with most perfectionists, she kept shifting the goalposts and so never felt good enough. She would obsess about whether she was a good daughter, and this led her to resent her mum because the relationship became a real effort. Veronica's mum hadn't said or done anything to create the guilt – Veronica had created it all herself; in fact, her mother didn't need her to the extent that Veronica believed. She was self-sufficient and, although she loved seeing Veronica, she only did so when she could see that Veronica was relaxed and enjoying the visit. If she sensed that Veronica was resentful and tense, her mother would actually rather she weren't there.

Through learning to communicate clearly and honestly (something that I will come back to at the end of this chapter), Veronica realized her mother didn't need her as much as she expected and she saw that she didn't need to feel guilty. It was as if a weight had been lifted from her shoulders and she was able to find balance in her life again. And, ironically, have a closer relationship with her mother as they enjoyed the visits and each others' company more.

It's quite common for a child to feel that their parents are disappointed with them when they're not and, as in Veronica's case, the child can actually create and project this guilt themselves. As damaging as this can be, it is far worse when family members intentionally cause guilt.

Case Study

When he was a teenager, Dan's parents often asked him for advice. They were going through a difficult time with their relationship and so turned to him for help, putting him into a really uncomfortable and unfair position. The roles of parent/child were totally reversed and Dan felt responsible for his parents' happiness. Unfortunately Dan's parents didn't work out their differences and got divorced, but rather than thinking about how they could make sure that Dan was least affected by it, they made him feel guilty about their split – particularly his mother. She would talk to Dan about her boyfriends, and when he started working and earning money she started to put him under even more pressure. She would have a go at him for not taking her on holiday and would hint strongly that he wasn't doing as much for her as he should. There was no sexual element to the issue but she made Dan into her quasi-husband and she made him feel guilty by putting unnecessary responsibility onto him.

This guilt inhibited Dan's ability to live his own life. He obsessed about being a good son and ended up developing social anxiety. His mum kept telling him that he wasn't good enough and so Dan believed that he was not only a bad son but also a bad person. He then generalized this belief to include his working life and the people he worked with, so he assumed that nobody thought well of him.

The reason Dan couldn't manage his relationship with his mother was because of her issues, but he couldn't see this because he took responsibility for her life and felt everything was his fault.

Now that I've explained to you the different ways in which insecurity can grow within the family environment, you may be wondering whether we are destined to be insecure as adults – or whether there is something we can do to counteract this.

The good news is that you can combat any insecurity, but to do so you need to step back from your family and develop a strong sense of self.

Ω Overcoming Insecurity and Fear of the Family

Insecurity about your family comes about because you hold on to what you perceive to be disapproval and continue to torture yourself with the expectations and pressure. So the ultimate aim in this recovery process is that you reach a point where you can see how family approval can make you feel good but where you can also ignore your family's disapproval. If you happen to get approval by doing what *you* want to do, then that's a bonus, but if your family disapproves you have to acknowledge that your approval of yourself is enough.

As we grow up, if we want to be secure in ourselves it's important that we learn not to care what others think. Quite simply, what we need as a child is diametrically opposed to what we need as adults. We have to shift our behaviour from seeking others' approval to seeking our *own* approval. It's healthy in teenage and adult years to draw away from the family, because if you never do this you never become your own person. You need distance from the powerful influence of your parents to give yourself a chance to grow into an independent person and have your own sense of self. This is quite ironic because the opinion of others, which is vital for human development in earlier life, is the cause of many insecurities later in life.

I'm not saying that it's not nice to be approved of by your family, and as an adult you can still get a feeling of warmth and love from being accepted and loved by your family. What I am saying is that this need for family acceptance has to take a back seat. It is healthier to get to the stage where if your family were to disapprove of you, you would be able to deal with it and get on with life. You can no longer allow your family's expectations to dictate your life. As hard as it may seem, to feel truly independent and have a secure self-esteem you have to be able to say *I am my own person*. The following steps should help you do this.

1 Get a sense of perspective

Try to give yourself permission to accept that while you really did need to depend on your parents when you were younger, as an adult you no longer have to take responsibility for their issues in order to guarantee their love. Remind yourself that your parents are human, too, and they have their own issues, insecurities and vulnerabilities. Even if you respect your parents you can still put yourself first some of the time.

Again, remind yourself that it is not your job to live your life as they would wish you to. It is not your job to fulfil your parents' dreams. It is not your job to make your family happy. It is not your job to live up to your parents' approval. It is your responsibility to make *yourself* happy. This won't mean that you have to upset your parents deliberately, but you are an adult and you have to live your life according to your rules. See that it is time you were your own person, and acknowledge this as a healthy and acceptable way to be.

2 Discover your own identity

More often than not, we find happiness by following our instinct. Nine times out of ten we know what's best for us, but if we don't have the courage of our convictions we tend to defer to what our parents think and assume that they know best.

To find out whether you are still living within the confines of your family script, take a pencil, paper and rubber. Draw a rough outline of a person – it doesn't need to be a work of art! Within that body write down at least 12 things about you. These may be things about your personality, such as 'funny', 'moody' or 'perfectionist'; your likes, for example, 'love rugby', 'enjoy reading poetry' or 'passionate about black-and-white movies'; and dislikes, such as 'hate politics', 'feel strongly about injustice' or 'get annoyed by rude drivers'.

Then look at each item and ask yourself: *Is that really me – or am I just fulfilling my family script?* There will be certain things that were 'set' as part of your family role that do feel like a part of you – and there will be some things that you know deep down you've just carried on with out of habit. If you want to reject any of these characteristics – rub them out.

When you've finished, you should be left with an image of you as you are – your own adult identity now.

By doing this exercise I want you to realize that you can love your family and still make different choices to them – and they can love you while not understanding your choices. You don't have to do everything in the same way and hold the same beliefs and values to be able to get on. You can all live your own lives and still be a family. Hopefully you will enjoy life so much more when you live on your terms and not anybody else's.

3 Stop the magical thinking

Support yourself to stand back from your coping mechanisms and think about how logical they are. Ask yourself: *Does flicking the light switch 50 times really keep me safe? Does never leaving my town limit me much more than it keeps me safe? Should I really be visiting my father every weekend? Is it my responsibility to look after my mum? Does this work or is this magical thinking?*

Magical thinking stems from childhood insecurity because you don't have the mental capacity as a child to know how to keep yourself safe. If you're not shown by your parents how to protect yourself, you end up using childish mechanisms and these can carry into your adult life.

To leave behind these obsolete coping mechanisms, take a piece of paper and split it into three columns. In the first column, write down what you currently do. In the second, write down what your motivation is for doing this: what belief do you have about this behaviour? In the third, write down how you would advise a close friend who wanted a new coping strategy. For example:

Old Strategy	Motivation	New Strategy
Flick light switch 50 times	To keep me safe	Tell myself I am safe, look after myself
Visit father every weekend	To be loved	Love myself by doing what I want to do at the weekend
Take my mother on all holidays	To gain approval	Acknowledge own approval by listing my achievements

When you grow up you know that there are better ways of coping, and knowing this can lead you to dislike and even hate yourself – but it is not your fault: don't beat yourself up because of what you used to do. Just as to an adult it's rational to avoid the rough part of town after dark, to a child it seems rational to flick the light switch 50 times – but now you are an adult you can adopt more appropriate ways of coping.

4 Use mantras

The final step in this process is about making your internal voice more positive.

To do this it really helps to find a set of mantras – positive statements about you and your life – that will help you cement your new beliefs. You may use sentences like:

I deserve to be happy.
I deserve to live on my terms.
I don't need to continuously care what my family thinks of me.

Or you can think of others that suit you better. Whatever they are, repeat these mantras every day until you believe them. These should help you to accept your new perspective and dispel the magical thinking you've been using.

Once you bring these four things together, you should be able to live your life as if you really believe you deserve it. As it becomes natural to think and act in this way you will eventually become more secure and will be able to enjoy a healthier, more balanced relationship with your family and yourself.

TAKE-HOME TIPS

1. Spend 5 minutes now writing out all the characteristics of your role within the family script. As you read back over these, if you feel something is inappropriate, cross it out. Write in its place the characteristic that describes who you are now.
2. Write all your achievements as an adult. Use this list to remind you of your identity and your strengths.

3. List all the things you're afraid of doing. Ask yourself whether these were things that were frightening for you as a child. Are they things that you should still be afraid of – or can you now, as an adult, move on from those fears?

ONE FINAL THOUGHT ...

Families may be a context for insecurities, but as an adult you have control over your own thoughts and emotions. You have the power to tell yourself that it's time to be free and that you genuinely deserve to be. The family does not have to be a context for insecurity unless we make it so.

CHAPTER 6

INSECURITY IN GROUPS

It is really important that I cover this form of fear, because we all experience this fear at some point in our lives. This is because humans are tribal animals. Through our evolutionary development we have lived in interlinking social groups, and we still do: at school, in our family environment, at work, through our hobbies, because of our political beliefs and values, and through our friends.

Groups are fascinating because everybody wants to be part of one and to have a sense of belonging. This drive stems from when we are first born and we needed to belong to our family because it was through their care we grew up and became independent: we literally had to fit in to survive. Then, as we get older, because we are social animals we still want to belong to a social group because this makes us feel positive about ourselves.

Our society is based on subcultures and groups, and everybody has their role and place in life. Over the ages we have grown to accept a set of social norms that dictate how we live. We have external restrictions that govern our freedom and we also restrict ourselves through our insecurities and internal conditioning. While we acknowledge the ideal scenario of success and happiness as coming from being the best we can be and being true to ourselves, in actual fact we are much more likely to keep our head down and blend in with everyone else.

We are programmed to want to fit in with society, so everybody conforms – either within the more acceptable conformist groups or the non-conformist groups. If you look, you can probably see all around you examples of people wanting to conform. You also only have to look at gangs of goths, punks or hoodies to know that these people want to stand out as being non-conformist – but ironically, by doing so they conform to their own subculture. Groups, in whatever form, dominate our society.

WHY DO GROUPS HIGHLIGHT INSECURITY?

With such a strong need to conform, group settings are a catalyst for insecurities. The group dynamics act as a mirror that makes us see our vulnerabilities, and this exaggerates what we perceive as our own shortcomings, because of how other group members react to us. For example, if someone is usually distant to us, whether it be a friend or family member or colleague, we tend not to wonder what is wrong with them; instead we often assume it is because of something we have done.

Case Study

Rosanne had a great life. She was a successful doctor, was happily married and had an active social life. One year her close group of friends decided to go on a diving holiday together. Everyone in the group considered themselves as sociable and warm, and they were also all good divers. Roseanne expected the two weeks to be easy and relaxed – but this didn't turn out to be the case. Roseanne found herself feeling very insecure, particularly in the first week of the holiday.

Roseanne felt that the other couples knew each other better than she and her husband did, and she started to feel left out. This insecurity was highlighted by the fact that one couple, the couple who were her closest friends and who had introduced her to that group in the first place, seemed to Roseanne to need to be the leaders of the group. Roseanne felt that they got some sense of validation by doing this, but because Roseanne wasn't naturally a follower her confidence was knocked and she took the odd bit of light-hearted teasing from the group as a personal attack. She felt she was being victimized, but because she wasn't used to being a victim she began to feel that she had to prove a point and began to be untrue to her identity.

She took a defensive position and began to be untrue to her identity. She tried too hard to make conversation and to compliment the leading couple. Roseanne knew she wasn't acting like an adult and she began to question whether she fitted in with the group or whether she was different. This made her feel very uncomfortable and inferior, and she then started to act in a needy way that made her more likely to stand out and be rejected.

For example, when they were buddying up to dive together, rather than be engaged by the marine life or concerned about how much air she had left, Roseanne was more bothered about whom she was partnered with. When they were arranging where to go for dinner, she was more bothered about being invited to the same restaurant as everybody else than she was about eating what she wanted to eat or going where she wanted to go. When they went to the beach in two cars, Roseanne analysed why she was in one particular car and, when they met in the bar for a drink, she would try to work out whether she could tell if people liked talking to her.

Roseanne was not used to being needy and she found herself obsessing and analysing every comment to try and read whether people liked her or not. Everything turned into an opportunity to work out whether she was being judged or accepted. She went from being someone who wanted to go on holiday to relax to someone who spent her holiday trying to get people to like her. She was missing the point of the break by obsessing about her social performance.

Roseanne was really upset by this and it made her think back to the time she had last felt insecure – during her adolescence. Roseanne found lots of parallels in the way she was acting, which is a very common reaction: she was saying things for effect, doing things just to be liked, and acting rebelliously by drinking too much in order to get noticed. She felt like she was going through an initiation into a select society, as she had when she was a teenager, and this made her feel stressed and upset.

If you want to finish this chapter feeling as if you totally understand this insecurity – and that you know how to combat it – you will be able to do this through the following exercise. It helps you bring on insecurity, not to upset yourself but to prove without doubt that you can overcome it.

Please don't do this at a time when you will have to be on form afterwards – for example before a meeting or before going out with friends. This exercise is going to show you how you can bring on a regressive state, so do this when you have time to relax and reflect afterwards. You also need to do the whole exercise step-by-step, because it is designed to be controlled and contained.

Ω *Understanding Insecurity*

1. Start by writing down what you're most proud of in your life right now. It can be anything to do with who you are: your relationship, how you look, your work, your home, the friends you have, something you've survived or the skills you have. Don't judge it – just write it down.

   Please note that if you can't think of anything, you are already somewhat insecure, so please don't do this exercise right now. This is really important because the aim of this exercise is to show people who don't feel insecure at the moment what it feels like, so if you're already there I don't want to make you feel worse.

2. Once you have something you're proud of, write down something you do in your everyday routine that makes you feel comfortable. This could be your walk to the

station, your daily run, your morning commute or the coffee shop where you buy your lunch. Write that down.

3. Next, think back to a time when you were made to feel insecure as a teenager. You may remember people laughing at your Doc Martens or your pixie boots, or talking behind your back about your hairstyle. It might be a time when you had bad acne or when you were self-conscious of your puppy fat.

4. When you have this memory clearly in mind, think back to how you felt. Remember what you were thinking, the emotions you felt and the physical feelings you had. Perhaps you flushed or felt sick in your stomach or had a headache.

    The chances are that when you felt this insecure you rejected who you really were and tried to conform with the very people who were making you feel insecure and persecuting you. So, although it may be uncomfortable, I want you to remember these feelings and thoughts in as much detail as you can: see what was around you at the time, hear what was said and relive the physical experience in your body now.

5. Now imagine you are feeling those feelings of insecurity with your current group of friends. Chances are you don't feel like this often with this group, but just transfer your adolescent experience of being an outcast to your current social group. See yourself colluding with them in a needy and vulnerable way.

6. Ask yourself: *How out of character does that make me feel? How does it feel to try to fit in? Am I changing to match the role I've been given?*

7. Now go back to the list you wrote at the start of this exercise – the things you've done that makes you feel most proud. Really engage with that: see yourself doing it and think about this until you feel positive again.

8. Next think of the second thing you wrote down – the routine you have or the thing you feel comfortable doing. Propel yourself back to the current point in time, to the stage of adulthood you're at and engage with your life and your mental state now to replace the memory of the insecurity.

Looking back at this exercise, realize how easy it was to feel insecure and be catapulted back to being an outcast. Notice how much more pain you felt because you knew that as an adult you should be able to act more independently. In addition, within a group this insecurity can be even more powerful because you have to deal with the added elements of other people's issues and interactions.

This experience can happen at any time: when you have to deal with a new work environment, when your child changes schools and you have new parents to meet, if you have a different boss, when you've got a challenging presentation to do at college – anything where you are thrown into a different group dynamic where your insecurities are allowed to come to light.

I hope this exercise shows you how everybody can feel insecure through the things we have to do every day. Being insecure does not make us weak – it makes us human. Where you can differentiate yourself and show your strength is in dealing with that insecurity.

'INGROUPS' AND 'OUTGROUPS'

Another thing I hope you can see through this exercise is that if you have been persecuted in the past, this was not because there was anything wrong with you: you were made to feel like an outcast because the people who rejected you were insecure about themselves. For example, if you were picked on for being immature, you may not really have been immature; rather, the people who put you down were actually insecure about their own maturity and they picked on you purely so they could feel better about themselves. They made themselves into what's known as an 'ingroup' and put you in the 'outgroup' to strengthen their position and confidence.

Case Study

When she was an adolescent, Louise was made to feel fat. One particular group of girls at school laughed at her and teased her for being overweight, so she started a strict diet and exercise regime. Because she was young, this worked really well. When she had lost a healthy amount of weight, apart from the group who had made her feel fat, everyone else acknowledged how much weight Louise had lost and said how great she looked. The group that had called her fat, however, still said she was too unattractive to be part of their group. Louise couldn't understand it.

Louise wasn't unattractive at all, but what she couldn't see was that it wouldn't have mattered if she'd ended up looking like a supermodel: to the 'ingroup' she was always going to be part of the 'outgroup'. They needed to ostracize a group of people – any group – so they could feel better about themselves. They were going to marginalize her and pick on her for any excuse they could find. Indeed, because Louise was so attractive, calling her unattractive perversely made the ingroup capable of deluding themselves they were amazing looking if they thought they were more attractive than Louise.

This case study shows how you can be picked on for any random reason: there is often no logic or truth to it and it's all to do with the insecurities and characteristics of what is known as an 'ingroup'.

Groups are formed on interaction styles. If you mix introverts with extroverts, because there isn't enough similarity within the group, rather than have total cohesion you end up with subgroups – one of extroverts and one of introverts. For example, when you're learning something at school or college you will tend towards a group that has a similar learning style. If you like to absorb material and self-reflect before you communicate socially, you will group with introverts. If, however, you learn best by discussing a new theory and sharing thoughts, you will gel with the extroverts.

There is no hierarchy with 'ingroups' and 'outgroups'. Whichever group you belong to will become your 'ingroup' and the other group will be the 'outgroup': there is no difference in status; the group's definition simply comes about because of your own belonging and so the labels depend on where you stand. One other thing I want to point out about these types of groups is that rarely are any of us always in one of the groups and, depending on circumstances, most of us spend time in both 'ingroups' and 'outgroups', especially during adolescence.

In adulthood, one of the most obvious ways of feeling like you're in an 'outgroup' is not speaking the same language as someone else. You can't even order a coffee or say 'hello' and so you feel like you don't belong.

When my husband and I were travelling around India, for one part of the trip we had to travel on a ferry. Women had to travel separately from men and I found myself feeling conspicuous and uncomfortable because I didn't speak the language and because I also looked different. These feelings were not alien to me but really highlighted to me that I didn't know this particular set of rules. I hadn't known that I couldn't travel with my husband, so I had to walk off the men's side of the ferry and get back on the women's part. I didn't know what was expected of me and how I should behave. I had become part of the 'outgroup' of one, just me.

This can also happen even in an environment when you *do* know what's expected of you. If something happens that makes you feel unsure of yourself, as soon as you question your security, that 'maybe' gets supported by any evidence you can find that you're different and that you are inadequate.

This happens to everyone at some point. We have all had this experience of worrying that what we believe about ourselves is not right. Having your self-belief knocked when you don't expect it can be a real shock and it can really throw you off-kilter.

Grouping happens across the board; it only causes problems when groups take on different statuses from each other. This may be through the rewards you get; whether these are real or psychological perks, they make the group dynamics very complicated. For example, the 'ingroup' can become the oppressors and the 'outgroup' can become the victims. This can be found in groups that are politically or racially oppressed, but this chapter is not about this kind of social situation. I want to focus on the type of insecurity that comes about purely through group dynamics – because this is what most of us experience.

THE TWO PATHS OF INSECURITY

When you're in the situation of feeling insecure in a group, whether it conflates your past and present together and catapults you back to adolescence or whether it simply exaggerates your current level of insecurity, there are two possible paths for you to take: the Insecurity Spiral, which makes you feel worse, or the Reframe, which helps you manage the insecurity.

The Insecurity Spiral

This is when you accept your position in the 'outgroup' and forget the reasons why you like yourself. You begin to criticize yourself for being 'rejectable' and end up rejecting yourself. This can in turn lead you to become depressed and defensive because you know you don't deserve criticism – either from others or yourself – and so you end up getting angry with other people and with yourself.

Once you're on this downward spiral it's easy to sink further and further. You'll look for evidence that you're being rejected whenever you're in a group, until eventually your criticism turns into condemnation. Social situations are no longer enjoyable, productive or constructive and life becomes lonely and depressing.

Ω *The Reframe*

This recovery process is all about challenging your insecurity, even if it started early in life. You remind yourself of all the things you're proud of now and all the ways in which you can see your worth. You see that you're no longer a teenager who's struggling to know who they are and to be accepted by others. You accept that you are an adult who enjoys your life, and you focus on this by reframing your position. Reframing takes four steps: seeing things as they are, challenging yourself, depersonalizing the situation, and rejecting the label.

See Reality
Rather than seeing everything as a personal attack, reframe your position within the group. This means seeing the evidence with a rational, unbiased eye. For example, if you're going on a daytrip and your friend doesn't have room in her car for you, it's not because she wants to exclude you: it's because she hasn't got enough room.

In addition, you need to realize that other people are not being hypersensitive to how you're feeling: the thought of rejection won't have crossed their minds, so they may then seem insensitive to you – it's because they're simply unaware of your emotional state.

Challenge Yourself
For every situation that you've taken to heart, ask yourself:

Did I mean to come across as aggressive/critical/immature/overbearing/insensitive?

These are just some of the reasons you may think the group might be rejecting you; your situation will be personal, so make sure you ask the right question. Whatever the question, if the answer is 'no', if it was not your intention to be that way, then why are you worried that you've done something to annoy other people? Why do you think you're to blame? When you can see *your* actions clearly, you can see *their* actions clearly: you didn't do anything to be rejected – and so they didn't reject you.

You can also ask members of the group about the situation. This is optional and I don't always do this in therapy, but in Roseanne's case I did want her to explore the group dynamics.

Case Study

I got Roseanne to ask her friends whether they thought she was immature and over the top. They all said that they hadn't found her immature and that they thought she was really good fun; but one thing that came out of the conversation, which Roseanne hadn't expected, was that a few of them were in awe of her: they thought she was really successful and so worried about what Roseanne thought of *them*!

In this case Roseanne's insecurity was fuelled by other people's insecurities, which she personalized – but she'd got it totally wrong! Once she realized this, Roseanne was able to carry on down the path of reframing because she could see that what she had perceived was wrong. She managed to regain her adult ego state, act rationally as she used to and be objective about her fear.

Depersonalize the Situation

It's easy to twist any piece of information to turn it into evidence of what you believe, but what you see as rejection is often just circumstance.

For example, if your friend didn't buy you a coffee it's because he couldn't carry another one. The group didn't exclude you from making a decision about where to eat dinner; they just went with what the majority wanted. You have to stop thinking that things like this are personal attacks against you.

Case Study

Roseanne was convinced her friends saw her as immature because this sparked a memory of when she was at college and had been ostracized for being immature and over the top. She actually wasn't melodramatic – the other girls were – so luckily Roseanne had been able to see this situation for what it was and had successfully reframed this insecurity. What she hadn't done, however, was recognize that this pattern might repeat itself and that she was unconsciously looking for evidence of being rejected again.

The evidence Roseanne found was actually nothing of the sort. She thought the group was rejecting her for being immature but, as she later found out, some of the members in the group were actually distant for their own reasons. One woman was worried about her job and had been preoccupied by this, so was coming across as distant. Another person in the group was worried about a member of his family who was sick, and so he was stressed and snappy.

Hopefully, you can see that you need to adopt the approach of a rational, assertive adult to depersonalize the situation. If you're not doing this you need to get yourself back on this adult path as soon as you can.

Reject the Label

If a past insecurity is causing you to feel insecure now, it's because your past and present are simply folding together – but the past is no longer relevant. Think back to that earlier time and realize that both you and the group were different then – and things have now changed.

For example, if you used to be seen as aggressive, look to see if you're still looking for the signs that people see you in that way. Are you projecting that onto them? If so, reject the label – and others will reject it too.

At every stage in this process, remind yourself of how you felt before you went into the group. Remember how strong and confident you were before the group dynamic threw you out of balance, and accept that the group has just been a catalyst for your vulnerabilities.

Ω *The Maintenance Process*

Once you've been through the process of reframing and you feel secure again, here's how you keep hold of that security, whatever situation you have to face.

1 Write down the following:

- things you've done that you're pleased with
- who you are as an adult
- what you like about your life.

Put this piece of paper in a safe place where you can see it often, and every time you have to do something difficult within a group – whether it's a tough meeting, a school reunion, a family gathering or a birthday party – read that list of things before you go. This will remind you of your strengths and your identity; you can then go into the group setting feeling secure and certain of yourself.

2 If you do start to feel relentlessly insecure, remember that everybody in that room is worried on some level about what other people think of them, so they're not thinking about you or anybody else. It's pointless getting hung up on other people's opinion of you, because you'll just waste your energy and won't get anything out of the situation.

3 Be yourself and know who you are. Do this by reminding yourself before you enter the group setting and, even if others act strangely around you or differently to how they usually would, just be yourself. This is very important, very effective and very workable to do.

TAKE-HOME TIPS

1. List all the groups you regularly encounter and how you feel when you're with them.
2. For the groups where you feel relentlessly insecure, do you have to see these people? If not, whether it's a work crowd or group of friends, make a decision to break away from this environment.
3. If you need to see this group, however infrequently, decide to act differently next time you see them. Use the Maintenance Process above to prepare you.

ONE FINAL THOUGHT ...

We have to be able to function in groups because groups

are everywhere, but while you can't eliminate insecurity as you can with other clinical forms of fear, you can control it; and it is by controlling it that you can free yourself from it. If you only ever stick to a routine because your insecurities are holding you back, you will only ever dread challenges; but if you face your insecurities and learn to manage them, you can truly live life with enjoyment and fun. I truly hope you can now see that it is possible to enjoy being in a group and still be yourself!

CHAPTER 7

SOCIAL INSECURITY AND ANXIETY

As you've read in chapters 3 and 6, it's very common to feel insecure around other people, whether this is a group or just one person. None of us is totally confident about who we are, so we all worry to some extent about what other people think of us. This level of self-doubt is an integral part of being human, but for most of us touches on only some areas of life and is, for the most part, manageable.

In some cases, however, this insecurity can become a much bigger issue. Some people are so afraid of being judged that their fear takes over their life and they become continually anxious about being around people, so much so they tend to adopt a relentlessly avoidant strategy. This debilitating condition is called social anxiety.

If you suffer from social anxiety it could be because you lack confidence in yourself. Perhaps you don't want to be near certain people or in a crowd because you think you're not good enough. Maybe you don't want to go to parties because you believe you're socially inadequate. It could be that you hate talking to your boss because you're scared of letting something slip that proves how poor you are at your job. Basically, you're convincing yourself – on both a conscious and unconscious level – that you're not good enough. This can affect your life in many ways because you don't let people get close to you, you feel you have to keep up a false public persona and you live in fear of being revealed as a fake, so you tend to withdraw.

Quite simply, this insecurity is based on the belief that you're not good enough as a human being. This may seem extreme when you see it written in black and white, but it is incredibly common: about 84 per cent of people briefly feel like this at some point in their lives.

Social anxiety can manifest itself as a specific fear, for example, a fear of crowds or a fear of authority figures, or just a general anxiety about interacting with others, but regardless of how it manifests, if you suffer from social anxiety it's because you are terrifying yourself with concern about how others perceive you. You second-guess what other people are thinking, make up the worst-case scenario and imagine that people are always being critical about you. But no matter how good you think you are at mind-reading, you can never really know what other people are thinking. So if your negative thoughts don't stem from the external reality, they must stem from your internal world – and are, in part, created through your self-talk.

A very strong internal critical voice is one of the defining features of social anxiety. This 'bully' inside your head guesses what other people think: *They think I'm ridiculous. They think I'm not good enough. They are laughing at me.* Then, because of this, it also dictates what you can and can't do: *I can't go to that party. I can't shop in that boutique. I can't give that presentation. I can't make that call. I have to stay in my job. I can't change.* Every time your internal dialogue says anything like this, you build up a greater body of evidence that proves how inadequate you are, so you become afraid of being around people because you can't face their negative judgement.

WHERE DOES SOCIAL ANXIETY COME FROM?

There are four reasons social anxiety can develop: prolonged insecurity experienced within a group; the generalizing of insecurity after one negative experience within a group; as a result of being abused; and from a very persistent critical internal voice.

I Prolonged insecurity within a group

By our very nature, we are social creatures. Whenever we use public transport, order something on the phone, buy a newspaper or even just walk past someone on the street we have some form of human contact: basically, if two humans cross paths, even if we don't say anything, we have a social interaction. But if you suffer from social anxiety, you genuinely believe that other people don't think you're good enough, so these daily interactions can become unbearable because you feel as if you're being judged relentlessly. Social anxiety can develop as a result of prolonged insecurity in any social situation, but particularly in group situations.

2 Generalizing one negative experience within a group

Social anxiety can also come about because of a negative experience at work, at college or at school where you were forced to be in a group, and within that group you were harassed, bullied, ostracized, victimized or unfairly treated in some way. Even if the treatment you received wasn't extreme, your *perception* of the group situation can make you develop social anxiety. You can then grow to dread not only that social interaction but also *any* social interaction. You believe that because one group of people looked down on you, everyone will. Rather than compartmentalizing that situation and putting it down as a one-off, you think that everyone will think you're not good enough. To protect yourself, you avoid being in what you see as threatening social interactions. You catastrophize and generalize that one negative experience and expect it to happen over and over again.

3 Abuse

If this kind of negative experience happens within the family environment it can be particularly problematic. You expect your family to love you, so if you have reason to think that they are criticizing or rejecting you, you usually end up thinking that nobody will want you – this is how abuse can be a cause of social anxiety.

There are other points in this book where I mention abuse, for example in chapter 5 on fear and insecurity in the family, so, although it is only a rare cause of social anxiety, I am going to take this opportunity to cover abuse. I hope that by doing so, if you've been abused or if you know someone who has suffered abuse, you will be able to gain a better understanding of it and realize that the victims are *never* to blame.

When people are abused as children, the abuser often explains to the child that the reason they're being abused is because they're not good enough; they justify their actions by saying that the abuse will make the child a better person. So the message the child receives is: *This is happening to me because I'm being punished for not being a good child* – but I want to reiterate and reassure you that this is *never ever* true. If you have been through this kind of abuse, before you read any further, please believe that you never deserved to be treated as you were. You were not abused because of who you are or what you did: so, whatever you were told, it was and is not your fault.

It's easy to understand the blameless position of the child from a logical perspective, but there is a rational explanation for why a child would take on the belief that they're not good enough. Evolutionary psychology deems that we listen to adults because we are born dependent on them, so we all grow up believing that what they say is right. So if you were told that you were being abused because you weren't good enough, and you were told this by someone who looked after you, it's understandable that you would believe it. It's also logical that you would use this belief as a foundation on which to build your fear of people in general.

This next case study is a good example of how the mindless comments of a parent can destroy a child's self-esteem and cause severe social anxiety.

Case Study

Janet was the product of an affair. Because of the pregnancy, her mother's affair came to light and, not only did her husband leave her, but her lover did too. Janet's mum was Catholic and kept her baby, and so Janet was born – but that was pretty much where Janet's luck ran out.

Janet's mum wished she'd had an abortion and took every opportunity to remind Janet of this. She blamed Janet for breaking up her relationship and she projected all of the guilt she felt about her affair on to her. She was also not prepared to take responsibility for what she'd done, and so convinced herself that she hated her baby girl. Janet was a sporty girl and her natural demeanour was happy and outgoing: she had a love of other people and wanted to take part in team games and activity groups, but the emotional abuse she received from her mother gradually dampened her spark and she became more and more introverted. This abuse was also highlighted by the fact that her mother went on to have two more daughters with a different father, so Janet was made to feel like the odd one out.

Janet's mum continually told her that she wasn't good enough, so even when Janet got an A in her maths exams or got a starring role in the school play, her mother would criticize her and put her down. One of Janet's most vivid memories was going to a birthday party when she was six years old. She got herself ready and put on her favourite pretty dress: when she went downstairs her mother said, 'I don't know why you're bothering to go. Nobody will want to play with you. Look at you – you look terrible!' Janet started to cry, as any little girl would, and assumed her mother was right. She must look awful and of course nobody liked her, so it was right that she shouldn't go. Not only did Janet miss out on the party: there were also repercussions at school. The girl who'd had the party was angry that Janet had snubbed her, and so she began to bully her; Janet had a very strong recollection of this but had not realized for many years how it was her own mother who had dealt the very distressing blow to her self-esteem.

All she was told every day was that she was not good enough, and this started to sink in. Janet had been born sociable and confident but her mother bullied her sociable nature out of her, and this left her vulnerable to even more bullying at school. It's sadly often the case that if you are the victim of one person's bullying, you become the victim of other people's bullying too. It's as if bullies can pick up on your vulnerability and this 'Kick-a-Puppy Syndrome' can lead to a lifetime of misery and abuse. Janet was rejected at home and at school; eventually she started to withdraw from social interaction.

As a teen Janet didn't like to be around groups or crowds. The thoughts that ran through her head were: *I'm not good enough. People can see that I'm inadequate and so the more people there are in a room or at a party, the more I will be condemned.* For Janet the presence of any other person was enough to trigger her feelings of inadequacy. Janet certainly didn't see a stranger as a potential friend: she thought a stranger was just another person who would persecute her, and so she went out of her way to avoid people. She didn't think it was possible for any human being to like her. She believed that everyone she met would dislike her and reject her because that was what had happened her whole life – even with her mother.

Janet's feelings also extended to a fear of authority. In her childhood her mother had been her authority figure, so she had learned that the criticisms of people who are superior to you have particular weight and power to upset you. This affected how she saw her teachers, lecturers and bosses. In spite of this, Janet did very well at university, proving that she had a strong survival instinct; she also saw education as her ticket away from her mother, so she worked hard and did well. She would avoid playtime by studying inside and her teachers were very kind to her, which made her study even harder: she didn't want to incur a teacher's disapproval because she knew how painful it was if someone disapproved of you, so she did everything she could to shine.

Janet drew her strength from her academic success, but when she got to university, her conscientious nature meant that she had hardly any time to mix with other students. When she did make friends, Janet never let them get too close to her; because she kept them at arm's length and believed she had to pretend to be someone she wasn't, Janet never relaxed. She couldn't see how lovely and likeable she was and that she was the kind of girl that people wanted to be friends with. Her loneliness only added to her pain. She was so afraid that by letting someone into her life she would be rejected – again.

At work, Janet was afraid of her boss and so she worked harder than everyone else and felt she could never say 'no' to anything. She took on extra projects and stayed late, and eventually reached burnout – that was when she came to me for therapy. She had never put her needs first. She had no idea what it meant to be assertive. She didn't like herself at all and told herself that nobody else liked her, either, so she constantly felt she had to compensate just for being herself.

Janet's story is a typical example of emotional abuse. In other cases of abuse, however, the terror can be even greater. The abuser will often tell the child that they deserve pain, humiliation, fear or even the threat of death and that they will always deserve it because they'll never be a good person. Often the innocent child can't work out what they're doing wrong, because as far as they're concerned they're doing everything right: they put away their toys, help clear the table, go to bed on time, brush their teeth, do their homework – yet still they keep getting told they're not good enough.

One of my clients who was physically abused couldn't work out what he was doing that was wrong. The only reason he could think of was that he didn't know how many grooves were on his bedroom wall; he thought that maybe if he counted them, the abuse would stop.

He didn't understand what was happening to him and desperately tried to find the reason why the very person who was supposed to love him the most was hurting him. So yet again you can see from this example that after years of being told you're not worthy and not being able to make sense why not, it's easy to go into adult life with very strong beliefs that you're inadequate, that something is wrong with you and that you should be afraid of people.

Abuse doesn't only occur in childhood: abuse as an adult, for example, domestic violence, can also be a cause of social anxiety. Whatever your age or gender, you can be made to feel as if you're not good enough, whether by your partner, colleagues or peers. Psychological abuse like this will also eventually lead to a negative belief system, because in a similar way to child abuse there comes a time when you've internalized the voice of your bullies for so long and to such an extent that you really believe what they're saying.

Because it's so traumatic and frightening, abuse can cause all of the fears in this book, including post-traumatic stress disorder and phobias. For example, a client of mine was sexually abused as a child. To numb her body and take her mind off the abuse, she used to stare at the pictures of rabbits on her bedroom wall; because she then associated rabbits with the humiliation and pain of being abused, she became phobic of rabbits.

Abuse in any form is horrific because no human ever deserves to be treated in an abusive way. We could say that the abuse does not fit the crime, but in most cases of abuse there is no crime at all: it doesn't matter how many pieces of Lego you left out, how short your skirt was, where you fell in the order of siblings, what grades you got at school, how badly you burnt the dinner, how messy the house was or what your gender is – you never deserve to be abused.

4 Internal critical voice

The final cause of social anxiety is a loud, persistent internal critical voice. In a way, this is also a form of abuse but it's not abuse at the hands of someone else – it's abuse at the hands of yourself. If you continually criticize yourself and tell yourself that you didn't do something right or that you're not good enough, you are basically abusing yourself by putting yourself down and negatively judging yourself, and you end up suffering from performance anxiety.

Most of us have some degree of performance anxiety about things like interviews, meeting our partner's parents for the first time, or doing unfamiliar things like travelling overseas: but if every time you do something – from saying 'hello' to someone to the way you walk into a room – you tell yourself you're doing it wrong, you become your own harshest critic. By condemning your every social interaction you eventually stop mixing with people altogether because this is the only way to avoid the self-bullying.

Apart from stopping you from interacting with people, in its most extreme form social anxiety can develop into agoraphobia. You can become so paranoid and afraid of interacting that you gradually withdraw from society until eventually you don't even want to set foot outside your front door: you end up sentencing yourself to a limited, lonely existence. To avoid this downward spiral, it's critical that you treat social anxiety and stop it before it takes over your life.

HOW DO YOU TREAT SOCIAL ANXIETY?

You can always treat and recover from social anxiety if you support and allow yourself to heal. You have to tell yourself that, although you may have been abused in the past, you're going to stop abusing yourself because you don't deserve it; you have to help yourself believe that, despite the fact you may have been afraid of one particular person or several people throughout your life, you're going to let yourself stop being afraid. Allow yourself to have hope and you can start again.

Let's start by working on the internal critical voice. This is based on internalizing the voice of your abuser or bullies. I'm going to try and help you help yourself turn that around.

When the words that are said to us are very powerful or cruel we start to internalize them and say them back to ourselves. If this has happened to you, try to realize you're not alone: this kind of situation is unfortunately common, but it is also reversible. Rather as we can get an advertising jingle stuck in our head, if you've been abused it is your abuser's voice that's stuck in your head – but it can be replaced by your own new, nurturing voice.

Ω The Treatment Process

The recovery process for social anxiety is all about self-validation: you have to change your belief system about how worthwhile you are. I will now take you through the six steps to becoming free of social anxiety and rediscovering your self-worth.

1 Become aware of your critical voice

To highlight your lack of self-esteem, the first thing to do is become aware of your critical internal voice. You can do this in a number of ways:

Keep a Diary

Write down everything that your critical voice says. You can do this either by getting a pen and paper now and thinking about the things you say to yourself each day, or you can carry a small notebook and pen with you and jot down your thoughts as they crop up. Be honest with yourself and don't censor that voice. Once you have finished, read them again: recognize how harsh they sound and try to tell yourself that you don't deserve this. Then, when you're ready, rip up the list.

The Chair Exercise

Put a chair in front of you and yell at that chair. Shout at it and say all the critical things you usually say to yourself. *Look at you! You're so fat. You're stupid. Nobody likes you. The slightest thing makes you fall over. You can't do anything. You're pathetic!* It may seem like an odd thing to do, but after a few minutes you'll start to believe that the chair is unsafe. It will look unstable and you'll feel nervous about sitting on it in future. That is what you do to yourself by constantly berating yourself: you debilitate yourself.

Invalidate the Criticism through Projection

Get a picture of a cute puppy or kitten, particularly if you're an animal lover, or nominate someone close to you to pick on. Say to that picture or person what you usually say to yourself – no matter how harsh or unkind. Don't be tempted to tone down what you say. Chances are you'll feel embarrassed about saying these things out loud, because you probably won't want to upset the animal or offend another person. You'll probably also be able to hear, perhaps for the first time, how wounding and how unfair these criticisms are. So why do you use them against yourself?

These techniques are really powerful because they are about self-validation. They show what's really going on inside your head and they also make you realize how powerful your bullying voice can be. You can do any one of these three exercises or, if you really want to attack your anxiety, you can do all of them.

This may be the first time you've become fully aware of your negative internal dialogue, so make sure you go easy on yourself. Don't judge – just observe. This is simply a behaviour you have learned, so now we're going to start unlearning it.

2 Believe you deserve to be happy

When you look at the criticism you've suffered – both external and internal – and you read the comments you've noted down on a sheet of paper, there must be at least a small part of you that can see that there is no way that you, or anybody else for that matter, could deserve to hear those things, as you are after all still a human being with rights. So this stage in the process is all about acknowledging your innocence and your right for a better life. The easiest way to do this may be to imagine that what you suffered actually happened to someone else. How would you feel about them? Would you think they were to blame? Or would you be reassuring and supportive?

The belief you have that you're not good enough is only a symptom of your fear; it's not reality. Sometimes when we do something naughty as a child we do deserve to be told off, or if we nag our partner it may be OK for them to get a bit annoyed with us: these are common, healthy examples of times when someone may have a bit of a go at us – but the horrific emotional and physical pain that comes from bullying is quite different.

It doesn't matter how mild or serious, or prolonged or short-lived your abuse, you didn't and/or don't deserve it. Now, I know you're probably reading that sentence and thinking, *I'm sure that applies to most people but I'm the one person who does deserve it* – but trust me when I say that you are no different to anybody else. You might wonder how I could possibly know that when I've never met you; but in all the years I've been practising, I have never met anyone who deserved to be the victim of a destructive negative internal dialogue.

You need to start working on the belief that you deserve to be secure, happy and confident, just like anyone else. You deserve to have friends. You deserve to have a social life.

You deserve to enjoy a career. You deserve to have a loving relationship. You deserve to meet new people. You deserve to be able to walk around in crowded places. All of these are things that most people take for granted as basic human rights – and you should, too.

3 Start thinking in terms of compliments

I said to you earlier on that compliments were going to feature heavily in this book – so here I go again! Liking yourself is critical to all of the recovery processes, and in my experience most people who are afraid or insecure are so used to being self-critical that they need to be reminded over and over again to be kind to themselves. I'm not going to lie and tell you this will be easy.

If you really don't know where to start, think about what you might say to someone else to make them feel good. Perhaps you'd say, *Your hair looks good. That colour suits you. You've got a beautiful smile. You've done a great job. It's lovely to see you.* If these seem too overwhelming you can start with something more moderate like *I look OK. I'm good enough. I'm all right.* It doesn't have to be over the top because you're unlikely to let yourself truly acknowledge it; it just has to be something you can comfortably say.

Once you know what you feel comfortable with, say that compliment to yourself every day – even if you don't believe it. Say it once a day when you wake up and then, after a week of doing that, say it twice a day – on waking and before you go to bed. When you hear these things more often, you'll start to believe them a tiny bit and then a bit more and then a bit more until you begin to grow more positive about yourself. Then you can start to say more positive things like *I'm a kind person. I'm good at my job. I'm really likeable. I'm a loving person* and so on until you begin to believe that you are worthwhile and deserve to be treated well.

When you're at this stage keep a list of all the complimentary things you say and aim to increase them. Just because you're saying kind things doesn't mean everyone will think you're bigheaded. Someone who has been relentlessly self-critical will never be arrogant, even though they often worry about it. Nobody has to hear what you say inside your own head and, if you think about it, nobody's known about all the criticism you've been giving yourself: your internal dialogue is for your ears only.

What you're doing by slowly changing the way you talk to yourself is changing your programming – raising the volume on your protective voice and dimming the volume on your critical voice. Because of some of the things you've been told by other people, you've simply got used to putting yourself down and worrying about what others think: now you can reprogramme yourself to be confident and comfortable with the idea of interacting with others.

4 Practise praise

Now that you've started to change your belief system and internal dialogue, you can adjust your behaviour to reflect these new thoughts: you can start attacking your fear on a behavioural as well as a psychological level. It's time to treat yourself!

Try to find four things you can do every single day that show how much you care for yourself. Perhaps run yourself a bubble bath; book a hair appointment; congratulate yourself on doing a great job on a project; take a walk; cook a delicious meal; buy yourself that CD or book you've wanted; relax in a yoga class. From the smallest treat to the most significant projects, all of these things indicate that you love yourself and believe you are worth it. This may seem like a lot to tackle, but everyone can do little things that make them smile.

Keep a diary of these four things because, by making a note of them, you can start to build a body of evidence that you *can* treat yourself well and that you *can* do so on a regular basis – and if your diary starts to look a bit bare, you know what you need to do: pay yourself more positive attention.

5 Discover your behaviour patterns

Next it's time to really crack your behavioural patterns. You've shown you can compliment yourself, that you can use a new internal voice and that you can even take small steps to look after yourself – but the only way that you'll know for sure that you're free of your social anxiety is to put yourself in situations that you'd usually avoid.

It's really important, however, that I make something really clear to you: We tend to repeat our behaviour patterns, so if we look at the example of abuse, if you had a very controlling, dominating father you are more likely to end up with an overbearing boss; or if you had an abusive mother you're likely to have relationships with abusive partners.

But you don't follow these patterns because this is what you truly deserve; it's simply what you know. You will tend to reach for what's familiar and what you think will comfort you – even if that thing or person is not a comfort at all – and no matter how negative the pattern, you will repeat it purely for familiarity.

The human need for familiarity overrides the negativity of the pattern even when the situation is painful and traumatic. I'm telling you this because I want you to realize that if you have been abused, when you start to expose yourself to the source of your fear – whether it's making new friends, having an intimate relationship, or opening up to someone – it's important that you know what pattern you have to avoid. I want you to get this process right.

Ask yourself the following questions:

What were the traits of the people who caused my fear?

Are there any similarities between them and the person I'm seeking out now?

List these traits and then keep a check on yourself. Seek to avoid these characteristics even if you think someone is right for you. Be honest with yourself even if it means spending a few uncomfortable moments thinking about the past and taking a long, hard look at someone who is close to you now. You owe it to yourself to do the right thing.

6 Expose yourself to the source of your fear

Once you are sure you are not repeating a negative behaviour pattern, you can begin the exposure. I'm going to take you through this process for the three most common social fears: fear of crowds, fear of authority, and fear of a family figure.

Fear of Crowds

If you are afraid of crowds I'm not expecting you to head straight off to London's Oxford Street on Christmas Eve, because very few people enjoy being squashed up against other people like that. What I do hope is that you can start by interacting with one person and gradually build up to more and more people until you can stand a crowded place.

The best way to do this so that you feel in control of the situation is to write a list of the steps you're going to take, and then take one step every week. Your weekly steps may be:

1. Go to the shops
2. Get on a train during off-peak hours
3. Go to the gym
4. And so on.

Every time you accomplish something, note it down and recognize that you are succeeding.

Repetition is the best form of defence for this kind of fear, so you need to keep doing things – different things – until they begin to feel normal.

Over time you will see that groups of people are OK. They are not going to harm you emotionally. They will not overwhelm you. They won't criticize you. They won't physically harm you. They are just other people who are going about their lives, as you are doing.

Case Study

Janet needed to interact with crowds but she needed to do this within her everyday routine. One of the things Janet did regularly was go to the gym, but she only went at quiet times when she knew there wouldn't be too many people around. So I got her to go at a busier time and eventually she went to a peak-time aerobics class.

When Janet started going to this class she believed that people would walk out just because she was there, so she tried to make every excuse not to go. *I'm tired. I should really stay late at work. I haven't got the right gear to wear. The class will be too full.* The first time she planned to go, she actually sabotaged herself by going the long way round to the gym so that she arrived too late to go in: but by discussing it with me, Janet was able to be honest with herself about having done that out of fear; the next time she went, she went with the intention of actually going to the class.

She said to herself, *It's OK. I can go. I deserve to do this. I'm not that bad* – and she got herself there. The first time she did this and nobody walked out, she realized that her imagination was worse than the reality. Janet could see that she passed lots of people without getting any negative judgements from them, so maybe there was no link between crowds of strangers and criticism. Maybe it wasn't true. Maybe she had made up this belief as a reaction to what had happened to her when she was little.

Fear of Authority

If you are afraid of people in authority you need to start by working out exactly whom you are scared of – and then you need to find a way to talk to them. Here is a step-by-step process that will help you face the person you fear; when you have a fail-safe formula to follow you can feel more insecure and put your focus on getting the steps right.

The Rules of Assertiveness (McKay *et al.*, 1983)

1 Take responsibility

Start your sentences with 'I'. This shows that you take responsibility for the situation. For example:

I have noticed that I am not performing as well as I could.

2 Define the situation.

Say how you see the situation so that it's very clear what you are talking about. For example:

At the moment I'm working on projects X and Y.

3 Say how you're being affected
Be clear about how the situation is making you think and feel. For example:

This makes me think I can't meet both deadlines and do both projects as well as I want to or as well as I can. This is making me feel worried and overwhelmed.

4 Suggest a solution
State what you think needs to change. For example:

I think I need to pass one of the projects to someone else. Alternatively I could complete both projects if the deadlines are extended.

These rules define assertiveness (as based on the theory presented by McKay, Davis and Fanning, 1983); if you follow them you won't come across as aggressive – but you will make your position very clear in a firm but measured way.

Some people have a fear of authority figures they don't ever have to actually communicate with, so you can tailor this step according to the person you want to face.

For example, if you are scared of the local shopkeeper, simply go into the shop, pick up what you want and, when you get to the till, look them in the eye, smile and say whatever you need to say – it may be a simple 'thank you,' but if this is the situation that you have felt unable to face in the past you have to expose yourself to it to be able to move on.

If your social anxiety is very serious, for example, if you also suffer from agoraphobia, start your interaction by answering the door to collect your mail from the postman or to pay your milkman directly. Next you can go to your local shop and interact with the shopkeeper. For most people these are little things that are simply a part of daily life, but to someone who has a serious fear of people these situations will be petrifying – so they are enough to begin the recovery process and achieving them is fantastic.

Family Members

If you are afraid of a family member, then you need to follow the same rules of assertiveness as above; in this situation, however, the stakes are somewhat higher because we're talking about a much more personal and potentially long-standing situation.

Here's an example of something you might say:

I've noticed that when you're having a family party, you don't invite me – but I'm a member of this family, too. This makes me think that either you don't like me or I've done something wrong, and this makes me feel very upset. I would like you to start inviting me.

If this person still doesn't include you, you have to realize that it is *their* issue: it is not your fault. When you're making such progress, you cannot afford to internalize this and take a step backwards. As painful or difficult as it may be, you have to cut yourself off from this person. You have to say, *I don't need this person in my life,* and you have to move on.

Case Study

Janet tried to talk to her mother and sisters. Her middle sister tried very hard to make it up to Janet and change the way she saw her. She realized she'd been following the family script and so decided to treat Janet as a friend and not as the bad person she'd been brought up to believe she was. But not all of Janet's family members were quite so understanding. Sadly, Janet had to cut her mother and older sister out of her life: they continued to make her feel terrible about herself and so she did the bravest thing by moving on.

By this point Janet was almost totally over her social fear. She was never going to want to go to a pop concert but she did start to throw dinner parties and she went to other people's parties, which were critical steps for her. After her childhood experience, it was really important for her to feel comfortable at parties.

Through this whole process Janet had to work on her confidence and realize that people liked her. By working on herself in this way on a continual basis, Janet was no longer living with fear.

For you to recover fully and get on with your life, you need to realize that you don't want or need people in your life who make you feel bad. You can no longer afford to believe that it doesn't matter how people treat you because you don't *deserve* to be treated well. You have to stop this way of thinking. You have to change. You have to tell yourself that it *does* matter how you are treated because, like everyone else, you deserve to be treated well. You deserve to be respected. You deserve to respect yourself. You deserve to lead a fulfilling and free life. But be aware that if you're used to being treated badly, you will naturally want to surround yourself with people who abuse you because that's what you're used to – but now is the time to turn that around. Break the pattern by only having people in your life who treat you as you deserve to be treated.

When you first start to do this exposure process you may feel convinced that everyone is looking at you, but this is just your imagination running wild. To see what's really happening around you, you must make yourself look up – literally. If you hold your head down you have no chance of noticing that most people are not looking at you, and if they are it's only because we naturally look at people who pass by: these strangers are not condemning you or judging you.

To help you keep a track of your progress, keep a diary of your interactions with people. How many people were on the train? How many people did you pass in the gym and in the changing room? What did you say to the man at the flower stall? What happened when you spoke to your mother?

By seeing that you can interact with significant numbers of people without being judged or experiencing any negative consequences, you can start to recognize that people are not judging you.

TAKE-HOME TIPS

1. Spend the next half hour taking notice of your internal dialogue. Just start to get used to acknowledging this voice.
2. Give yourself three compliments by the end of the day.
3. Plan four nice things you can do for yourself tomorrow. Write them down on a piece of paper or in your diary so you commit to them.
4. Write down on a piece of paper or a Post-it note: *I am not a fake. I am good enough. I deserve to like myself. I deserve to be liked.* Put this somewhere you can see it (maybe stick it on your mirror or by your bed) and read these sentences every day – whether you believe them at first or not.

ONE FINAL THOUGHT …

When you start working through this process you will become your own best friend and will begin to realize that you didn't deserve the way you were treated. You may even find that the abuse was actually to do with the other person and their issues – they just took it out on you.

As with all the fears in this book, the reality is never as bad as you imagine it to be. You won't let yourself down. You don't need to be afraid of yourself. You can and will be among people because you deserve to be and are good enough.

CHAPTER 8

ANXIETY

Anxiety comes about because you believe you are utterly incapable and not good enough and that at every turn there is a threat to your wellbeing. Anxiety is based on stress, fear and self-doubt becoming literally overwhelming. You feel unable to make decisions, to control your body or thoughts and generally to function properly. Because of this inability to function you can't think well of yourself and believe that nobody else can think well of you, either.

Most fear is directed towards a concrete external object or situation, but with anxiety there tends not to be any concrete thought pattern behind the emotion: anxiety just takes grip without any apparent cause or reason. It stems from our experience – our own internal world – and not from the external environment. For example, you might be reasonably afraid of not being able to pay your mortgage because you've just lost your job and interest rates have gone up; or you may lie awake at night feeling anxious that you can't make your mortgage payments or pay any of your household bills even though you have just received a hefty bonus and a pay rise. The first is an example of rational fear, the second is irrational anxiety. Perhaps you're afraid your partner might leave you because you know they've been seeing someone else, which, although devastating, is an example of fear that has a real cause. On the other hand, you may be sick with anxiety because you're convinced your partner's going to dump you even though they've just proposed. That's an example of anxiety that's been created in your internal world.

As you can see, anxiety is different from fear; it is also distinct from worry. Worry, or concern, is an inevitable part of everyday life and it can be appropriate and reasonable. We're human and so we will worry from time to time. Worry tends to be short-lived and relatively mild in comparison, and when you're worried you are still able to cope with your life. When you're truly anxious, however, your negative feelings are so debilitating that you can't continue with the routine of life: the anxiety stops you functioning as you would wish.

In some cases of anxiety you can't understand what's causing you to feel anxious but what you do know is that the feeling is very intense, it affects all areas of your life and it won't go away. There is no rational trigger like an unfaithful partner or a massive credit card bill: instead your anxiety is generalized, which means that you start to feel anxious about anything and everything. If you suffer from anxiety you will also catastrophize situations, so while other people can't see what the big deal is, you feel like it's the end of the world, your thoughts are often about impending doom. This kind of anxiety is often described as *free floating* (Bourne, 2000), which means it is a vague yet persistent and pervasive feeling of uneasiness. It seeps into every corner of your life and follows you around.

Case Study

Olivia's anxiety started by coming on only when she was at a party. This is a pretty widespread and rational social worry and lots of people feel uncomfortable with the pressure of having to be exciting and interesting, especially if they're with people they don't know. But Olivia wasn't just a bit worried – she was anxious. She suffered from all the usual physical signs of anxiety: racing heart, dizziness, palpitations and sudden sweats – but as well as these acute physical reactions, which only came on when she was in a social situation, she was also suffering from chronic hair loss, which made her feel even more self-conscious.

Over time Olivia became anxious in every social situation – even if she was just out having dinner with her boyfriend. She was scared of losing control of herself and dreaded what other people would think of her if she did. She was even afraid her boyfriend would leave her because she was convinced he was put off by the fact she couldn't cope. Olivia also generalized her anxiety to the point where she was paranoid about what people at work thought of her and she believed she could no longer cope in her job. Her anxiety had gone from having a rational trigger – the social pressure of parties – to become less and less context-specific until it pervaded every aspect of her life. She could not function normally and felt she no longer had control of her life.

Anxiety is all about your ability to trust yourself and therefore the belief you could easily let yourself down or lose control. You feel as if you have no control over your mind or body and no control over your environment, so you constantly feel in danger. The truth is that you have got control but you just don't believe it. You can't make sense of what's around you and so can't function within a social context. You experience feelings of impending doom, and worry that you're going to die, even when there's very little chance of this happening. This is due to feeling so concerned and therefore so vulnerable that you really worry about what else might go wrong. Understandably you feel you can't cope with any more stress, so you panic about possible future stressors. For example, you may see on the news that there's been a natural disaster on the other side of the world, and become convinced it will happen to you. Or when you partner leaves the house, you might worry that they'll die in an accident. Or you believe that because you feel you can't make rational decisions, every decision you do make will be the wrong one. You may believe that there is a conspiracy against you, so, for example, if you decide to accept a job offer you'll be convinced the job will turn out to be the wrong one for you and will ruin your career.

This kind of self-torturing thinking can also apply to smaller and seemingly insignificant decisions. So you may get up one morning and choose to wear a particular jumper; if you then decide that you've made the wrong choice, you relentlessly berate yourself for not being able even to get your choice of clothing correct.

The world that the anxious person inhabits is a very hostile place. It's a world full of self-doubt and self-loathing. It's a world where you continually have to face tests that you will not let yourself pass: success is not an option. Everything is exaggerated and becomes a catastrophe. This is particularly harsh because when you are already stressed you pile on even more stress.

Say you're driving along a smooth, dry road and there is no traffic. You haven't been drinking and you feel alert. There is no logical reason why you might crash – but you're convinced that you will. You drive along with a sense of impending doom and you keeping saying to yourself, *I'm going to crash. I'm going to crash. I'm going to crash.* You can't give a specific reason for your fear because there is nothing to be specific about. It's not raining. It's not dark. There are no other drivers around to hit you or to suddenly brake. There is nothing external to trigger your anxiety. There is no danger – and yet you still feel unsafe: that's when anxiety has taken hold of you.

Case Study

When James came to me he was really embarrassed about a fear he'd developed over the previous few months about which he didn't feel he could speak to anyone, not even his wife. When he was driving, James would suddenly be gripped by the fear that he had run over someone. He never felt a thud and never saw anyone come near his car; he had no rational reason to believe he'd hit someone but he was petrified that he had and hadn't noticed.

He was so terrified that he could take someone's life and end up in prison that he started to adopt obsessive-compulsive behaviour: he kept stopping and getting out of his car to check. This was so disruptive that it would often take him three times as long to get anywhere. He would even check the traffic news to see if there had been any hit-and-run accidents on the routes he'd been driving; if there were any, he would be gripped by a paranoid and intense fear that he was guilty. When he came to see me, James was on the point of going to the police to admit to a hit-and-run that he hadn't done. In his rational mind he knew he hadn't, but his anxiety was so great that he feared he had.

HOW DOES ANXIETY AFFECT YOU?

Olivia's and James's stories clearly show how anxiety affects your whole being. On a psychological level you feel like you have no control and you go about your life with a sense of vulnerability: you talk negatively to yourself and feel detached from yourself. You might even think you're going crazy. On a behavioural level you change what you do to accommodate the anxiety; you avoid anything that might feel stressful and therefore, sadly, limit yourself. Finally, on a physiological level you experience rapid heartbeat, dry mouth, excessive sweating, queasiness, muscle tension and hair loss and, in the most serious cases, you might even think you're going to die.

To someone who doesn't suffer from anxiety this might seem terribly melodramatic and a bit of an exaggeration, but it really can happen and is more common than you might think. It can happen to anyone and can feel very hard to deal with, so people who cope with anxiety are actually incredibly brave. In fact most of us will feel stressed to the point of anxiety and self-doubt at some point in our lives.

Case Study

Almost every night Tim would wake up a couple of hours after he'd fallen sleep. He would have a tight throat, his heart would be beating wildly, he felt dizzy and he would be gripped by an intense fear that he was going to die. Tim wasn't ill so there was no specific trigger for his fear, it was simply a free-floating fear that his life would end. He would wake up shaking and had no idea why he felt the way he did, so he would pace his living-room floor trying to get a grip on himself. The only conclusion Tim could come to was that he must have a heart problem, so he convinced himself that he was about to have a heart attack.

He went to see a heart specialist who performed a series of gruelling medical tests but she found nothing wrong with Tim. The specialist suggested that Tim consider the possibility of psychological causes – she said this even after the first test but Tim was having none of it. He hated the thought that he might have a mental problem and would rather believe he had a physical problem that he could really understand.

It's quite common for someone to be in denial about their anxiety. Many people believe that there is some sort of stigma attached to psychological disorders. There shouldn't be any stigma: emotional and mental health problems are part of life and can affect anyone. People who suffer from anxiety also often feel bewildered and confused by the fact that it's intangible, so by turning it into a tangible heath problem they feel they can understand it.

However, it's important to acknowledge and deal with the anxiety before it takes root and grows. If left untreated, what starts out as a seemingly harmless level of anxiety can develop into something else as well, such as panic attacks and, in some cases, even a phobia. Like a drop of ink that spreads across a tissue, a minor concern or a seemingly insignificant incident that if left unresolved can develop into full-blown anxiety that colours every aspect of your life.

To prevent this from happening to you, I want you to understand that curing anxiety and sorting out your own mental health *can* be a tangible process. There are people who can help you and it's not something you have to put up with. If you ignore it and work your life around it, you risk developing a long-term disorder. So, if you are suffering, I hope you will feel compelled to do something about it.

THE ANXIETY SPIRAL

One of the things you can do to help you see your anxiety as a tangible thing is to work out what *level* of anxiety you have. I believe that anxiety has four levels of intensity:

Level 1: Mild anxiety – a sense of general uneasiness

Level 2: Persistent anxiety – as above but relentless

Level 3: Paranoia-inducing anxiety – the fear that something is going wrong inside you, for example, the belief that you're going crazy

Level 4: Acute panic – a sense of impending doom and a feeling that you can't cope.

While all levels of anxiety are unpleasant, if you have a continual feeling of imminent serious danger, like death, that's when anxiety has really taken hold and you must get help for yourself. You don't have to live with it: you can eliminate it.

Anxiety can be broken down to a scientific level of understanding and, in a similar way to a physical disorder, can be treated in proven and standardized ways. Anxiety may be invisible but the symptoms and resulting effects on your life can be *felt* and *seen*. By working out where you're at in the Anxiety Spiral you will see that it is a real experience that can be categorized. Once you realize that you can literally grab hold of the problem, you will feel empowered and able to fight it.

WHAT CAUSES ANXIETY?

The two key causes of anxiety are a traumatic incident or situation and an enhanced and relentless critical self-talk. Often they are found together because you experience something traumatic and then keep on torturing yourself with catastrophic thoughts about it.

Critical self-talk is not to be confused with schizophrenia or auditory illusions or 'voices inside your head': we all have our own self-talk. Here are some simple examples that we can all relate to. When we get dressed in the morning, we look in the mirror and ask ourselves, *How do I look?* We don't say it out loud – we say it inside our head. We walk down the street, see a coffee shop and ask ourselves, *Do I fancy a cappuccino?* When we're getting ready for a meeting, in our head we prepare by talking through how we want to come across and what we want to get out of the meeting: *I must make sure I clarify the time-frame of the project and whom I'm reporting to.* We self-talk all the time – it's just what humans do – but with anxious people the difference is that their self-talk tends to be continuous and seriously critical.

Case Study

Tom was a high performer. He had a very responsible and powerful job and a stable and loving home life. But despite seemingly 'having it all', Tom constantly thought he was going to mess up. He gave himself a really hard time and could only see a future of disaster and doom. He felt he would be abandoned or rejected by his wife when she discovered that he wasn't a good person; he thought that his employer would find him out to be a fraud; he believed that everyone would eventually see that he was not the person they thought he was.

This all came to a head when Tom started planning a trip to do some aid work with his wife in Cambodia. His negative thoughts began to spiral out of control. *I won't be any good at the work and I'll make it worse for those I'm trying to help. I'll show people that I can't cope and I'll be thought of as a failure because I will have failed the people I wanted to help. I will also let my wife down. So I can't be a good person and I can't have any morals because I'm scared and a moral person wouldn't be scared...* and so it spiralled from a manageable level of concern into a mass of anxiety and fear. When the time came to leave, Tom couldn't get on the plane – not because he had a fear of flying but because he had a fear of failure. His anxious thinking had become so catastrophic that he was swept up in a negative landslide and couldn't see a positive outcome for anything.

I asked Tom to write down all the outcomes he could see, and to rationalize them for me. I wanted to know why he thought these things might come true. Why did he think he wouldn't be able to help people? What made him believe he'd look like a fake? What was the process that led him to believe his wife would think he was a failure; When I forced him to look logically at his tendency to catastrophize everything, Tom realized that he had no reason to believe any of the outcomes he had imagined; in fact, all of his experiences to date, both personal and professional, formed strong evidence that he was very well suited to doing a fantastic job as an aid worker and he was a very well-loved and worthwile person.

This inability to engage with the positive things in life is one of the most common factors in anxiety. As is the case with many anxiety sufferers, Tom needed to engage with his anxious thoughts to realize that they were not true.

Someone with anxiety often has a negative commentary running inside their head: *Everyone's looking at me. I can't do this well. Nobody wants me here. Nobody likes me. I'm not good enough. Everyone's looking at how much I'm eating. I'm putting people off their food. Everyone thinks I'm a hassle. All my friends hate me.* So if you're always giving yourself a hard time and saying, *I'm terrible, I'm terrible, I'm terrible,* it's inevitable that you'll start to believe and completely accept that you really are a terrible person.

It's natural human behaviour to give yourself a bit of a hard time now and again: for example, if you've put on weight, when you look in the mirror your self-talk will probably say, *You're looking a bit fat,* or if you're on a date in a posh restaurant and you knock over your glass, sending red wine all over your dinner, a voice in your head will say, *I can't believe I just did that!* If you drop a clanger with your in-laws about the black sheep of the family that nobody's supposed to mention, your critical voice will say, *You've really put your foot in it this time.* These are all situations where, no matter how strong your self-esteem, your inner voice will jump at the chance to remind you that you're not perfect – and that's quite common because none of us is perfect. But when this voice takes over and all you ever hear are destructive comments, that's when self-talk can create psychological disorders.

If your internal dialogue is very extreme it will make you edgy and paranoid until you eventually believe the things you are telling yourself. You will believe that you can't cope; that the outside world is dangerous; that your internal world is dangerous; and that your whole existence is insecure and harsh – and that's how something that starts as a few critical comments can turn into an anxiety disorder.

HOW DO WE DEVELOP A CRITICAL INTERNAL DIALOGUE?

Self-talk that is this unhealthy and negative can develop in many ways: through our communication with our parents or childhood carers; in abusive adult relationships; through nature and nurture; as a result of drug use; because of a particularly strong negative experience; and through prolonged everyday stress. Basically, if we have developed a low self-esteem we will develop a critical internal dialogue.

1 In childhood

One of the popular topics of discussion nowadays is self-esteem, but what do we really mean by that? To have robust self-esteem you have to know deep down that you are OK; that even if you sometimes make mistakes you're a fundamentally good person. You believe that even if you're not perfect (nobody ever really thinks they are perfect) you are worthy of support and, as a result, you will have a nurturing internal voice. But anxiety comes about because of a fundamental lack of self-belief. Without this basic level of confidence in your abilities you can develop a deep-seated conviction that you're wrong or that you're a bad person.

This conviction can often have come about because of the messages you were given as a child. If a critical parent always tells a child that they've done something wrong or that they have to do things differently, that child will eventually believe they can't do anything right. If they're told that they're clumsy and their mother says, 'Don't carry that drink – you'll spill it,' or 'Don't pick that up. You're bound to drop it,' they will focus so much on what they're being told that they will end up dropping things, spilling things, falling over themselves and becoming clumsy. There is a high likelihood that this child will then grow up to be an adult who tells *themselves* that they always get things wrong – and because they're so convinced that they can't do anything right they will go on to develop anxiety. Repeated criticism becomes a self-fulfilling prophecy.

Sometimes the criticism doesn't even have to be verbalized – it can also be picked up through visual cues. You may remember from the earlier chapters on insecurity that the first time in our lives when we consider who we are and how we're seen by others is at about the age of two: we look into the eyes of our primary carer and we read how they perceive us through their smile and the glint in their eyes. It's hard to quantify this definitively, but through the research that's been done, developmental psychologists believe that this is when we first begin to develop a sense of self-belief. We might be able to read from these eyes that we're lovable, or that we're essentially good – even if we make mistakes: but we can also pick up messages that we're not loved or not worthy – all from a look.

Because at such a young age our primary carer – whether it's our mother, father, a grandparent or someone else – is the most important person in our life, we absorb their opinion of us and make it the foundation for our own belief in who we are. So if you weren't loved and protected when you were young, you may have grown up feeling as if you can't protect or love yourself, because you unconsciously believe you don't deserve it.

2 Abusive adult relationships

A critical inner voice can also start within an adult relationship. If you're in an abusive relationship where you're criticized by your partner all the time, even though you're more self-aware than a child you can still start to internalize and believe the critical voice until, eventually, you become your own bully. Even if you move on from the abusive relationship and find a loving, supportive partner, it doesn't matter what they say to you because your own self-talk has become so loud and persistent that your inner critical voice overrides any positive comments you may hear.

Abusive relationships can also happen in the workplace in the form of harassment or bullying. This usually needs to be over a sustained period of time, but it can lead to you taking on the criticisms of others and forming your own critical self-doubt.

3 Nature and nurture

People are more likely to develop anxiety if they have an anxious parent, because when they were young they looked to their parent to learn how to respond to the world. So if you saw your parent being anxious, you would not have had the maturity or awareness to realize that what they were doing was inappropriate: you would believe that the situation was genuinely terrifying and dangerous and therefore something to be anxious about. It's very hard to say for sure whether you can inherit the condition from your parents but, as with most things in life, it's likely that if you have an anxious parent and you too are anxious, you picked this up through a combination of nature and nurture.

4 In response to drug addiction

Any type of drug that alters the way the synapses in your brain communicate to produce feelings of euphoria can go wrong and cause the brain to develop feelings of paranoia. Most people have heard about the risk of growing paranoia as a result of taking recreational drugs, but you can also develop anxiety if you see something that really worries you while under the influence of a drug.

Case Study

In his late youth Jack had been involved in the hardcore rave scene. One night when he'd taken his usual Ecstasy pill, just as the drug was beginning to wear off and he was coming down, he saw someone being taken away on a stretcher. He thought, *That could be me if I forget to breathe!* This developed into *Oh my god, I might forget to breathe!* And so Jack focused on his breathing so that he wouldn't lose control and forget to do it.

> From the moment he saw the person on that stretcher Jack became paranoid about breathing; then this generalized until he'd built up a belief that he had to focus on his breathing to stay in control and to stay alive. He started to believe that he wouldn't remember to breathe unless he consciously thought about it.

We can't live without breathing, so because Jack focused on something that is fundamental to human survival, something that we usually do unconsciously, he gave himself the critical message, *I am not even good enough to be able to breathe on my own.* Jack was undermining his very humanness and so developed self-doubt about his ability to keep himself alive. As a result he began to feel overwhelmed and to think that he wasn't safe in the world. That one stimulus while under the influence of drugs led to six months of anxiety.

5 A strong negative experience

Another cause of anxiety can be a negative experience that gets generalized, in a similar way to a drug-related experience, into omnipresent anxiety. The following case study demonstrates this really well.

Case Study

> One of my clients, Clarissa, went to a work party and got very drunk. The next day she had a vicious hangover but had to go into work for a departmental meeting; in the

middle of the meeting she was sick. As much as this wasn't an appropriate thing to do, it was an understandable response to having had a serious amount of alcohol, and even though it was embarrassing, Clarissa's colleagues had all been at the same party. But Clarissa was mortified and became convinced that she would be sick, not just after alcohol, but any time she went into a meeting.

This experience had been so negative that Clarissa then generalized her anxiety into not being able to trust herself at all in public situations because she thought she might throw up at any time. Her critical voice said, *I can't trust myself. I'll throw up and embarrass myself. I can't keep control of my body.* Her internal voice told her over and over and over again that that's what she was going to do. Eventually, after several weeks of repeatedly telling herself the same damaging things, Clarissa lost all ability to trust herself.

6 Everyday stress

Stress is an integral part of our lives and most of us experience it to some degree, but if it happens every day and becomes overwhelming, anxiety can develop. What starts out as the odd challenging day when you can't see how you're going to fit everything in becomes a hectic week. This turns into weeks of stress which become a relentless period when you've got too much to do, you're working too hard, you're not getting enough sleep and you fail to take care of yourself. You then begin to worry you can't get everything done and the little reminders that you used to say to help you remember everything become a running commentary of self-doubt. *I won't get that done. I'll forget to do that. I'm not going to get this right. I have to finish that. I've got to work on this.* This negative self-talk sows the seed of self-doubt regarding your ability to cope. Over time, if there is no let-up, this seed grows into everyday stress. Over a prolonged period (around fourteen months) this everyday stress, coupled with nagging self-doubt, can become anxiety. Other names this is known by are 'burnout' or a 'nervous breakdown', and it's more common than you might think.

THE TREATMENT OF ANXIETY

When it comes to treatment, you have to remember that even if you have a serious degree of self-doubt, you can cope with life. You don't *deserve* the way you treat yourself. You haven't *caused* it. You're not *overreacting.* You're not *weak.* You're not being *pathetic.* The hard time you give yourself is both the cause of the problem *and* what makes it persist, so if you want to overcome it you have to change the basic belief that you *can't* cope into believing that you *can.*

If you're reading this and you have anxiety, please take this in:

> *I am good enough.*
> *You don't deserve it.*
> *Most importantly, you can cure it.*

Say it like a mantra:

I am good enough. I don't deserve it. I can cure it.

Say it even if you don't believe it. When you've said it 20–30 times every day for weeks on end, you *will* start to believe it – but you have to persist. Once you've done this you're ready to follow the three-step recovery process.

Ω *The Three Steps to Overcoming Anxiety*

1 Challenge Your Critical Voice

Whatever the cause of your anxiety, one factor that appears in every case is the negative inner voice. Your critical voice will eat away at your self-esteem until you no longer believe you can cope with the world. You can dismiss your self-talk as *Just stuff you say to yourself* or *The same stuff everyone else says*, but if the way you speak to yourself is unnecessarily punishing or destructive, you will eventually erode your self-belief and your sense of self to the point where you can't function in a healthy way.

To get over your anxiety, you have to confront your critical self-talk. But before you do this you have to realize how powerful that voice is – and work out what it's saying.

Here's the same exercise from the last chapter that demonstrates the power of the critical voice.

The Chair Exercise

Put a chair in front of you and shout out all the critical things you usually say to yourself. *Look at you! You're terrible. You're weak. You haven't got the strength to stand up. You can't do anything. You're pathetic!* It may feel strange, but really let yourself go and, after a few minutes, you'll find that you start seeing the chair as unsafe. It will look unstable and you'll feel nervous about sitting on it.

I know this might sound a bit silly, but if the way you see that chair can change in a few minutes, imagine what damage you can do to your self-esteem if you beat yourself up day after day, week after week, month after month and year after year. When you make yourself mentally unstable through your self-criticism, you make yourself feel unstable and insecure.

So now that you're hopefully ready to work on your internal dialogue, you need to work out what that voice is saying. Write a list of all the things you say to yourself. Once you have this list, ask yourself: *Would I say these things to a child?* I'm guessing you wouldn't: you know it would destroy a child's self-esteem – yet you destroy your own self-esteem on a minute-by-minute, day-by-day basis.

Your critical voice does not dictate what you do and you cannot afford to listen to it: it will simply feed your fears. The good news is that you can quiet that voice and learn to speak to yourself in a positive, life-affirming way. You don't have to believe what it says. You have to stop thinking that this voice speaks the absolute truth; instead, see it simply as the voice of your disordered irrational thinking. You have to question the validity of what it says. You have to talk back to it. You have to believe you can get rid of it. By answering back to this voice you will start to realize that it doesn't speak the truth: it's just part of your anxiety – and it has to go.

The best way to start talking back is to get a rhythm and routine to the technique. Choose three mantras that you find empowering and motivating. You can use the three statements I gave you earlier:

I am good enough. I don't deserve it. I can cure it.

Or you can vary them:

I'm OK. I am safe. I can beat it.

Or you can choose phrases that are more specific and personal to you. To give you some examples, let's look back at the case studies in this chapter and see what each of these clients said to themselves.

- Olivia, who was anxious and self-conscious in public situations: *I am good enough. I have a right to be here.*
- James, who was convinced he had run over someone: *I can keep on driving. I know I haven't hit anyone. I have nothing to be afraid of.*
- Tim, who was convinced he had a heart problem: *I don't have a heart problem. I can go back to sleep. I can calm myself down.*
- Tom, who was anxious about his overseas trip: *I will do a good job. I am good enough. I will help people.*
- Jack, who was anxious over his breathing: *I can breathe automatically. I've been doing this my whole life. I can do it.*
- Clarissa, who was scared of being sick in public: *I am in control of my body. I am calm. I won't be sick.*

Choose phrases that work for you. Keep them by your bed or in your wallet or anywhere else where you can see them every day. Over time, your mantras will seep into your mind, help break down your irrational thought pattern and start to rebuild your ability to think logically and calmly.

Unfortunately you can't wave a magic wand to make this voice go away – there is no ON/OFF button for our internal dialogue – but if you do this exercise several times every day, the voice will start to fade and will eventually disappear.

2 Calm the Physical Symptoms

Apart from hair loss, which is a chronic symptom of anxiety, all the other acute symptoms can stop immediately. They are all related to breathing, so they can be controlled by learning to breathe in a calm and slow way.

When you slow down your breathing your brain receives the message that everything's OK; there's no need to run away; there's nothing to be afraid of; as a result less adrenaline will be released into your body. With less stress hormone whizzing around your bloodstream you enter into a calm physical state, and this is when the positive cycle of recovery can begin. Your body feels calmer so you are less likely to feel in danger. Your critical voice then stops telling you to feel threatened and so you continue to feel calm and the cycle starts again.

The Home Position

Here is an exercise that you can do anywhere, at any time, to help you to breathe more deeply and slowly. I call it

'The Home Position' because it's a way of taking yourself to a safe and familiar place no matter where you are.

> Sit with your feet flat on the floor. Have your legs hip-distance apart. Hold your arms out in front of you at chest height as if you're holding a big ball. Interlink your fingers and make sure you hold your arms loosely in the circle formation. If you're in a public place, you can put your hands on your knees so it looks as if you're sitting quietly.
>
> Keep your eyes open (although you can close your eyes so long as this doesn't make you feel dizzy) and look at your fingers with a soft gaze. Then start to breathe in and out through your nose and count your breaths: In… for Two… Hold… for One… Out… for Two… Hold… for One… In… for Two… Hold… for One… Out… for Two… Hold… for One… and so on until you feel your breath start to slow.

You must remember that, even if you feel self-conscious, there is nothing unusual about The Home Position and you can do it anywhere. There is nothing eye-catching about it, so nobody will be staring at you or judging you. It's really important that you do this because it will teach your body how to be calm and, each time you do it, it will become easier and easier until it becomes automatic.

3 Change Your Behaviour

To treat your behavioural symptoms you have to stop

joining forces with your anxious thoughts – and this means changing your actions. You have to stop doing the things that have started as a result of your anxiety and turn them on their head. You do this by creating new habits that literally displace your anxious behaviour. As before, let's look back at the case studies to see how each of these people changed their behaviour:

- Olivia changed her body language. She stopped hunching over and started to stand tall. She stopped censoring what she said and just spoke up.
- If James got the urge to stop his car, he told himself that there was no thud so he had no reason to stop: he made himself drive on.
- Tim stopped having medical checks. He faced the fact that his problem was not physiological but psychological and, when he woke up, he made himself stay in bed. He told himself he didn't have a heart problem and he lay still until he fell back to sleep.
- Tom organized another trip as a volunteer. He planned in advance all of his techniques for managing his anxiety and visualized himself doing it.
- Jack stood tall and didn't allow himself to focus on his breathing. He knew that it would happen automatically.
- If Clarissa started to think about being sick, she would adopt The Home Position and repeat her mantras. She pictured herself healthy and did this until the thought and feeling passed.

While it may seem hard to stop doing something that feels compulsive, the things you have been doing when you're anxious are just behaviours that you've learned. Even if you didn't learn them deliberately and you only started doing them in reaction to the anxiety, the fact that you learned these behaviours means that you can unlearn them. You never used to do them so you can go back to how you were before your anxiety started.

These three steps are all about recognising you can be and are in control: of your thoughts, your body and your behaviour. While some of the techniques seem small, they work – but you need to practise them consistently. It takes six weeks for anything to become a habit, so if you do these three steps for six weeks, you will start to condition yourself to think rationally and to believe that you can cope. These new thought patterns will help you let go of your anxiety and so, by working through this process, you will win back control of your mind and body and will start to understand where your anxiety comes from. You will then gradually get your life back in balance.

TAKE-HOME TIPS

1. Spend five minutes visualizing how you would like to feel and how you would like life to be if you were free of your anxiety. Decide to do this for five minutes every day this week.
2. When you have been through the visualization enough times to feel as if you really can do it, when you next visualize, find a way to anchor your body to this positive state: click your fingers or squeeze your fist.

3. Say to yourself every day, *I can be this person. This is me.* At the same time, fire your anchor – so repeat the action of clicking your fingers or squeezing your fist – to induce that state.

ONE FINAL THOUGHT ...

Anxiety does not develop overnight: it develops cumulatively and it's cured through cumulative action. Each time you talk back to your critical inner voice, you chip away at the anxiety. Every time you embed a new behaviour, you train yourself to stop reinforcing the old anxious thoughts. Every time you breathe deeply, think positively or act differently, you start to rebuild your self-esteem – and this is fundamental to overcoming anxiety. Over time, with patience and practice, you can win back your freedom and return to a psychologically healthy, rational and protective place.

CHAPTER 9

PANIC ATTACKS

We've all had really stressful days when we want to hide under the duvet and wish the rest of the world would go away: but imagine if that was your life every day. Imagine if the only place you felt protected and in control was underneath your duvet; and that if you had to face anything or anyone, you believe you'd fly into a panic. Perhaps this kind of fear reaction is at the more extreme end of the panic spectrum – but whether you experience panic for several weeks or for just half an hour, it is always a petrifying feeling.

What Is a Panic Attack?

Panic attacks are basically the physical manifestation of anxiety, but I've devoted this chapter to them because I feel that the physical symptoms can be so debilitating and frightening that they need to be singled out and dealt with on their own.

The common physical symptoms are: dizziness, shooting pains up your arm, tightness in the chest, blurred vision and auditory perceptions, sensory overload, hyperventilation and excessive sweating. When you read this list you can see why many people mistake a panic attack for a heart attack, though even after they have been given the all-clear by a doctor many panic-attack sufferers will still fixate on physiological disorders rather than facing up to the fact that their condition is psychological. You may remember this from Tim's story in the last chapter on anxiety. Tim used to wake up in the night thinking he was dying but he was so concerned about the stigma attached to having a psychological problem that he preferred the prospect of having a heart condition.

One of the most frightening things about acknowledging a psychological condition is coming to terms with the fact that your thoughts and feelings can really affect your physical body. But our head is attached to our body and so it's inevitable that *what* we feel emotionally will affect *how* we feel physically. If we feel angry we might get a rash; if we feel stressed we could get eczema; many people who are anxious have digestive problems. All of these are common examples of how thoughts and emotions have a direct effect on the body. Panic attacks are just another physical symptom of your mental state. They are simply a combination of emotions that are so overwhelming that in the moment that they come together they are able to induce physical symptoms powerful enough to be sometimes mistaken for medical conditions. But ignoring the signs is not the way to deal with the fear. Neither is avoiding the trigger.

Those of you who don't suffer from panic attacks may find it hard to relate to these behaviours and symptoms, but it's important to remember that we must never judge someone for what causes them stress or for what they can or can't do as a result. People who have panic attacks are just as capable as anyone else: they just *struggle* with what they have to cope with. This doesn't mean that they *can't* cope – it means that they occasionally get overwhelmed; and this feeling of 'overwhelm' will probably happen to all of us at one time or another.

Case Study

Michael worked in a fairly stressful job in the safety standards industry. His responsibilities included giving small presentations and holding meetings, and he felt relatively confident about these roles. The one thing that Michael didn't feel happy with, however, was giving presentations to large groups of people. If he had to address more than 100 people he would start to shake and sweat profusely. He was so worried that people could see him shaking, even though it was only a slight tremor, that he over-focused on the shaking. This then made it worse and so Michael would start to flush and hyperventilate and his symptoms would eventually lead to a full-blown panic attack. Michael felt so overwhelmed by the physical signs that he was convinced he would faint, which is not uncommon for sufferers of panic attacks.

Large group presentations make lots of people feel a bit anxious; but the problem for Michael was that he couldn't avoid them. To progress in his career he had to give presentations: he knew he was good at his job and could go higher up the ladder and he wanted to be promoted. But unfortunately, because he didn't deal with the cause when it started, Michael began to generalize his trigger to include the thought of doing any presentation.

In the run-up he would become worried and analyse his panic in such depth that just by imagining a presentation he could bring on an attack. Instead of thinking rationally along the lines of: *If I panic I'll deal with it. I won't worry about it. I'll just get on with my job,* he thought: *Everyone knows I struggle with presentations. I'm going to panic. I won't be able to continue. I'll look really stupid. Everyone will think I'm a total idiot and I'll lose my job. I've got to get out of it.* He focused on his fear and so it intensified, and what started as panic in his mind became panic in his body.

Panic attacks are often stigmatized in our society but they *are* real reactions, they *are* terrifying and they do what they say on the tin: you do suddenly get taken over by a barrage of frightening physical symptoms and it does literally feel like an attack. Your breathing starts to change and you feel out of control; you think you're going to pass out or have a fit. If you've never had an attack before, you probably have no idea what's going on and you might wonder whether to call an ambulance: this can make you feel even worse. Once you've started to have panic attacks, you are also likely to have them more frequently, which makes you worry about when they might hit. You wake up every morning and think, *Will I have a panic attack today? Will I have two? Will today be the day that my attack makes me collapse? Will I be able to cope?*

When you're experiencing panic attacks they are a real struggle to come to terms with but, as much as they may seem to take over your body, you can overcome them.

I don't mean to oversimplify the process because fear is undoubtedly a complex subject, which is why I've decided to write this book; but while it's not *easy* to understand and control panic – it is *possible* to change the way you respond in order to overcome it.

One of the most important things to remember when you're dealing with panic attacks is not to overreact and say, *I'm going to give myself a heart attack. My heart's going to give out. My head's going to wear out. I'm going to become ill.* None of that is true. It's important to acknowledge but not overreact to the signs and say, *It's not a big problem. They'll just go away. I'll be fine.* So, when you feel a panic attack coming, take a moment, sit down and let it wash over you and then tell it to slip away.

You will see later in this chapter that the key things to remember when treating panic attacks are: acknowledge them, understand them, then control them. It may seem overwhelming to try to understand why you react the way you do, but by breaking the process down and ordering it in a logical way I am going to help you become rational and measured. You have to teach your brain that you can cope and do so in a manageable, safe and gradual way. By reading this book you have taken an important step in acknowledging your fear and that, in itself, can be a challenging thing to do.

WHAT CAUSES PANIC ATTACKS?

There are two main causes of panic attacks and they are both psychological. They are terrifying thoughts and self-doubt.

1 Terrifying thoughts

Panic attacks are simply the physical embodiment of your thoughts. They are not caused by something in your environment; they are caused by your *response* to something in your environment. Panic attacks don't come from out of the blue: they are created in your head. If you are really terrified about something and worry obsessively about it, you will feel emotionally overwhelmed – and this will trigger the physical reaction of panic. The thinking always comes first – and then the panic attack. In some cases, usually the most extreme ones, the mental starting point is very hard to detect because the physical symptoms start so soon afterwards that the mental and physical responses seem to be simultaneous – but the thought *always* comes first. So it's crucial to remember that no matter how overwhelming or scary the panic or how out of control you feel, it has been caused by your thinking – so you can stop it through your thinking. You have the power to control your panic attacks by changing how you worry about a situation.

2 Self-doubt

Self-doubt is not an external thing that's separate to your being. It's not like a virus that you catch or an object that you pick up and carry around with you: it's an internal process that affects the whole of your being. You might start by doubting your ability and thinking, *I can't do this*; over time and as you think this more often the thought becomes so strong that you begin to believe it. You frighten yourself by imagining the consequences of not coping until the fear grips your body – and it's that self-created fear that leads you to become physically disabled with panic.

Self-doubt crops up in all cases of insecurity, anxiety, fear, phobias and panic attacks because it is the underlying cause of any form of fear. To be free of fear you have to banish any unnecessary negative beliefs that you can't cope or that you're not good enough.

Case Study

To return to Michael, he already knew that he panicked in large group presentations but by working together we managed to pinpoint the specific cause. Michael panicked when there was some serious consequence riding on the delivery of his presentation: either he had to get across an important message about a project, he had to secure more business for the firm, or he was being assessed for promotion.

What all of these things had in common was that Michael's communication skills had to be strong enough that he could change people's opinion. He worked in the safety standards industry so it really was important that the standards and methods he was communicating were adopted because if not, people's lives were potentially at stake. So when he felt that the point he was making was critical to the safety of others or when the presentation was pivotal to his future, Michael began to panic about his effectiveness and performance – and this led him to doubt himself. As his attacks became stronger, so he trusted himself less and less.

The Treatment of Panic Attacks

Most people's method of dealing with their panic is to avoid the situation – like not giving presentations, or getting their shopping delivered so they don't have to go to the shops, or taking the bus instead of the train – but avoiding the situation will only maintain your fear: by not dealing with the root of the problem, the trigger can then be generalized. This was very evident in Peter's case study in chapter 2 as he grew his fear from being afraid of tube trains to being afraid of anything with a tube symbol on it.

By not dealing with the cause of your fear you can restrict the way you live your life – sometimes to the point where your life is dominated by strategies to avoid your trigger. Some sufferers limit their lives more and more until just leaving their house can induce an attack and so they create a life that is severely restricted. Avoidance does not work: it may keep you in your comfort zone but it will never free you of your fear and it gives you the message you have to hide yourself away because there is something to hide from, when there is not.

Don't give yourself the message you can't cope and that you need to run and hide: you *can* cope and you *can* face the fear.

The key things you have to do to get rid of panic attacks are to control the fear and not allow your thoughts to be continuously catastrophic.

Control the Fear

The fearful response we have that triggers panic attacks is different from the fear response that our bodies were designed to have. The original fear response was created to protect us from real physical threats like lions, tigers and bears. When we felt afraid, our body would release adrenaline, which got us into a pumped-up state for action. The extra strength and focus this gave us was then used to 'fight or flee', which was totally appropriate: if a seven-foot bear was headed straight for you, you'd be grateful for the extra power in your muscles so you could run like crazy. But we no longer have the same dangers in our lives and, as clever as our bodies are, they have yet to adapt this evolutionary response to match today's environment.

Modern fears, like the fear of giving presentations, a phobia of paper clips, anxiety brought on by train stations and fear of spiders, are all situations that don't require us to be pumped-up and fit to fight; to deal with them we need to be in the opposite state – calm, controlled and balanced. Your body doesn't know this, and that's why you have to learn to stop your body's natural reaction by changing the way you think. If you train your brain to feel less threatened, it won't trigger the extreme fear response, and so the panic attacks will slowly stop.

Banish Negative Thinking

There's nothing wrong with negative thinking – it's simply a thought process that takes away your confidence: so don't judge yourself harshly for having negative thoughts, because we all have them some of the time. That said, if your negative thoughts have been taking over your life, now is the time to give yourself a break. Acknowledge that you're being brave by facing an emotional topic which, quite frankly, you'd rather ignore. Give yourself some credit and praise for focusing in a rational way.

Now you have in mind these two main factors, I'm going to take you through the four-step treatment process.

Ω Step 1: Identify the Cause of Your Fear

Panic attacks are treatable if you acknowledge them and get to the root of the problem. Even if you're not aware of what the cause is, by working logically backwards you can find it. Once you have this root cause you can get started on the recovery process and analyse the rest of your thoughts.

Like all of the fear responses in this book, to eliminate panic attacks you have to think calmly about the psychological factors. Some people resist thinking about this because they confuse it with obsessing – but it is completely different. Obsessing puts an intense focus on the fear and maintains it, but thinking calmly and rationally disempowers your fear because you see it for what it really is. As long as you learn to control your thinking and keep it directed, you *can* identify the cause of your panic attacks.

Think about your fear when you're feeling calm and in a safe place. Never do this when you're in the middle of a panic attack or if you're in a place that triggers your attacks, because you need to be able to think clearly, calmly and rationally. When you're feeling ready, think about what it is that makes you feel afraid of the situation. For example, if you get panic attacks when you go to the shops, ask yourself, *What is it about the shops that makes me feel afraid? Is it the people in the shops? Is it the buildings themselves? Am I frightened of things in the shops? Am I scared of interacting with other people?*

More often than not, people's fear and doubt stem from what they believe other people will think of them. They think that people will judge them because of how they look, what they say or what they do, and so they start to think, *I'll embarrass myself. I'll do something stupid. Everyone will look at me.* I don't want to put ideas into your head, but if you can trace your way back to the root of your panic and you're still not sure of what it is, check to see if your underlying concern is what other people might think of you.

Case Study

It took us a while to pick out the root of Michael's fear. To do this he worked back in his mind through every step of his fear, rather like rewinding a videotape or DVD in slow motion. We found that his fear stemmed from the thought, *I don't know if I can do this.* It might seem like an innocent statement, but because Michael said it over and over again to himself, it infected the whole of his thought processes and behaviour.

To make sure you completely get rid of your panic attacks, you have to knock down the first fearful thought for the rest of your behaviour to cave in. It's like knocking over a row of dominoes: if you don't hit the first one straight-on, you only knock a few down and the rest are left standing – and by the end of this process you don't want to be left with any remnant of your panic. The way you do this is by creating empowering thoughts.

Ω Step 2: Create Empowering Thoughts

Without even knowing you, I know that you have told yourself for a long time that you can't cope – and that's because everyone I've worked with who suffers from panic attacks is well-practised at putting themselves down and telling themselves they can't do something. You *have* to turn this belief on its head – and you do this by telling yourself over and over again that you *can* cope and you *will* be OK. The most effective way of doing this is through mantras. Here are some examples of positive mantras:

I can do this. I won't embarrass myself. I will be able to cope.

The first time you read these you might think, *There's no way I can do that* – but read them again and then write ones that are specific to you. Once you've identified the thoughts you need to change and the mantras that work best for you, you need to say the latter five times a day, regardless of whether or not you've had a panic attack or even whether you're going to have to face your fear. No matter how little you believe them, look in the mirror and repeat your mantras again and again and again. Over time you *will* start to believe them: even if only 1 per cent of you believes them, it's a start and everything has to start somewhere. Say your mantras first thing in the morning – out loud, if you like – and then get up and get on with whatever you have to do. That's less than a minute of your time every day, which is a tiny investment for a happier future.

My clients often get overwhelmed by the thought of changing their thinking and they say to me, *I can't do it any more. I don't remember how to control my mind. It's been too long* – but there is no time in our lives when our brain's physiology changes to the point where we can no longer control our thoughts. We can always change how we think. You may be out of practice with controlling your thinking, but you can do it any time.

I'm not guaranteeing that this is going to be easy, but mantras can make you feel empowered and if you're really determined to be free of your panic attacks, you have to be patient and chip away bit by bit at what has, for a long time, seemed like an insurmountable challenge. Remember that your panic stemmed from words and thoughts, so you have to use words and thoughts to overcome it.

Case Study

Together Michael and I created mantras that suited him. He felt most comfortable with:

I am a good communicator. I can do this. I am calm.

He put these on a Post-it note on his computer screen so that even on the days when he wasn't presenting, he could still take a few minutes to work on feeling more powerful.

Ω *Step 3: Visualize Yourself Coping*

The next step is to work out what to do when you're faced with the cause of your panic attacks so you can control the physical symptoms too. In a similar way to training your brain to think positively every day and not just when you would usually think negatively, I want you to practise coping when you are not in a panic situation, and I want you to do this every day until you feel confident that you can do it for real.

See yourself coping in the situation. Imagine feeling calm and in control. Use all your senses to work through that ideal situation in your mind and see a successful outcome. Do this over and over again until it starts to feel very real – as if you really could do it.

Case Study

Michael saw himself walking up to the podium feeling confident. His hands were steady and he could calmly look out into the audience. He imagined speaking in a measured way and then walking back down off the stage feeling confident that it had gone well. He practised this visualization several times a day. Whenever he had a quiet moment, he would run through this ideal scenario until it began to feel very real.

Practice is essential. Imagine if you were driving somewhere and you were in a rush: you might know that there was a different route but you wouldn't try it when you were under pressure. You'd wait for a day when you were feeling calm and had all the time in the world. Don't wait for a real panic situation to try out your new behaviour: practise first.

Ω *Step 4: Control the Physical Symptoms*

You've identified the cause, started to change your thinking and have visualized yourself coping and staying calm in your old panic situation. Now you have to practise controlling your physical symptoms. I took you through this process in the last chapter, but it's so important that I'm going to repeat it. As with the visualization and mantras, you need to practise being in a strong physical state when there is no risk of you panicking.

The Home Position

Sit on a comfortable chair with your knees hip-distance apart. Hold your hands gently in your lap. Look straight ahead and make sure your shoulders are square on and down. Close your eyes (unless you have a tendency to get dizzy when you close them) and begin to control your breathing by counting. Breathe through your nose In… for Two… Hold… for One… Out… for Two… Hold… for One… In… for Two… Hold… for One… Out… for Two… Hold… for One… After four cycles, open your eyes and do another four breath cycles. Remember you cannot hyperventilate when you're breathing through your nose.

It is physiologically impossible to faint while you're having a panic attack. So you should just keep breathing through your nose, but if you're in the throes of a fear-induced attack you can feel very starved of oxygen. So if after eight cycles of breathing in and out your breathing is not slowing down, use your hand to cover your mouth to ensure that you are breathing through your nose.

> Take one hand out of your lap and put it over your mouth, being careful not to cover your nose as well. This will force you to breathe through your nose. Carry on breathing as before. You can do this even if you have a cold – just breathe more slowly. Keep your eyes open, otherwise you may feel too closed-in.

It's important for you to realize that by doing this you're not denying yourself oxygen, you're just slowing down your breathing. It will not harm you – it will help.

> Once your breathing has slowed, put your hand back in your lap.

> After the eight breaths, keeping your body comfortable, start to say your mantras. You can also add: *I am gaining control. I'm physically in control. I'm control of my thinking.*

> Open your eyes (if they've been closed) and look down at your hands. Relax your eyes. Don't be tempted to look around you – stay focused on your lap.

This is what you do to control the physical symptoms. Practise this at least 10 times before you try using it to control a real panic attack.

The first time you use this technique in a real panic situation will be the hardest. But when you've done it once you will have hard evidence that you *can* do it; so when you next feel an attack coming on, you will feel more confident. You've done it before. You've practised the drill over and over again. You know what to do and you *can* do it. Over time you will build a whole body of evidence to prove that you *can* cope: you *can* control your thoughts and you can calm your body. **Note:** You can use these techniques in conjunction with the processes for facing any fear or phobia, but bear in mind that you also need to do the specific work detailed in the relevant chapter. You cannot do one without the other.

TAKE-HOME TIPS

1. Whatever you are doing or wherever you are, take a few minutes now to practise breathing in a calm way. Breathe in and out through your nose, counting each in- and out-breath for two slow counts.
2. Say to yourself, *I am a calm person. I am in control of my panic.* Try to say this out loud in front of a mirror.
3. Remind yourself that you can feel calm whenever you next have a panic attack.

ONE FINAL THOUGHT ...

It's unlikely to happen overnight, but when you practise

the four-step treatment process you will eventually stop worrying about the attacks. Your self-doubt will diminish and you will no longer need to beat yourself up. You will start to trust yourself, and when you trust yourself and stop worrying, the panic attacks will become less intense and less frequent – and there will come a day when they will have totally disappeared from your life.

CHAPTER 10

PHOBIAS OF OBJECTS

WHAT IS THE DIFFERENCE BETWEEN A FEAR AND A PHOBIA?

Phobias are conditions that are at the very extreme end of the fear continuum, so it can be hard to distinguish a phobia from an intense fear. My definition of a phobia is 'a persistent unreasonable fear of a specific activity, object or situation that results in a compulsion to avoid the dreaded object, activity or situation, or anything reminiscent of it'. That's a very formal definition, so let's take a look at what it means in practice and how a phobia differs from a fear.

Three things differentiate a phobia from a fear:

1. A phobia is something you dread so much that the most important thing to you is avoiding it.
2. You are terrified of any representation of your phobic object and of anything that even reminds you of it – so for example, if you are truly phobic of mice, you would be as petrified of real mice as you would be of a picture of Mickey Mouse.

3. You may believe that your phobic object has a nasty intent towards you, as it can feel as if the phobia is personally attacking you.

To show the difference between a phobia and a fear, I have chosen spider phobia (or arachnophobia, as it is also known) as this is a very common one. It belongs to a group of phobias called *atavistic* phobias. Atavistic phobias are phobias that have at one time been evolutionarily appropriate: so, in the case of spiders, many hundreds of thousands of years ago these creatures, and other creatures like reptiles, snakes and amphibians, posed a genuine threat to our survival. Nowadays these animals no longer threaten our existence, but some of us are left with a fear of them.

Looking at the first feature of a phobia, if you are phobic you will organize your life around what you see as potentially threatening situations. You are constantly on the lookout for signs of danger – even when you know it's irrational – and you arrange your life to avoid being anywhere near your phobic object. Here are some spider-related examples:

- One of my clients had such a strong spider phobia that she left her baby alone in the house for five hours because there was a spider on the front door step.
- Another woman couldn't even say the word 'spider' and was paranoid that a species of spider that was only found in Australia would make its way over to the UK to get her.

In the case of other phobias, if you're phobic of buttons you will only wear clothes with zips or ties and won't even have buttons in your house. If you have a phobia of dogs, you will feel terrified that one will come bounding out of nowhere to attack you. If you're phobic of birds you could feel too scared to leave your house in case one comes swooping down from out of the blue.

As for the second defining feature of a phobia, a phobia is so intense that even thinking about the phobic object can cause the physical manifestation of the fear, such as sweaty palms, shortness of breath, shakiness, dizziness, tinnitus, stomach tension and nausea. Some people are so phobic that they can't even verbalise whatever it is they're frightened of and call it 'the S word', in the case of spiders. Someone who is phobic of spiders will experience the same fear response from a photograph of a spider or from saying the word 'tarantula' as they will from actually being near a real spider.

The third distinguishing factor of phobias is that phobics believe that the object of their fear has some horrendous intent. So, in the case of spiders, a phobic wouldn't just see a spider as something unpleasant that might crawl on them but as a creature who wants to go out of its way to hurt or frighten them.

One of my clients had a phobia of mice. When she saw one on the platform of the tube station she was convinced that the mouse was specifically trying to stop her from getting where she needed to go. She was so terrified that she made a dash to escape and had to be stopped from accidently running in front of a train. She believed the mouse had a malicious motive to do her harm. She knew it wasn't logical, and in her rational moments she knew it wasn't possible for a mouse to hurt her, but, as with all phobics, when she thought of her phobic object, her thinking became irrational and focused on catastrophes.

Phobics have usually been afraid for a long time: On average, the phobics I've worked with have lived with their phobia for 12 years. They have had a long time to consolidate their fear so that it becomes impossible to get rid of by themselves. Part of them knows that their phobia isn't logical, but the part of them that gets gripped with fear genuinely believes that the threat is real and imminent.

Although this may sound strange to non-phobics, it really shouldn't. Phobics are not less intelligent than other people; in fact, they tend to be creative. They are aware that most people don't share their fear, because they have got a rational voice. On another level, however, they see their phobic object as something harmful. Because of this seeming irrationality, there is often a stigma attached to being phobic, especially if your phobia is unusual – like a phobia of door handles, cheese, safety pins or fruit. Some phobics are ridiculed because they're afraid of something that is inherently not scary and because they have a different reaction to the norm. Because of this stigma, most phobics end up giving themselves a hard time, but as you will have seen in all the chapters, self-deprecation only serves to maintain fear.

THE THREE TYPES OF PHOBIA

There are three main classifications of phobia, grouped according to how they are caused – by trauma, by conditioning, or as a result of a projected fear.

Phobia caused by trauma

This happens when one specific traumatic event changes the way you see a particular object. It may be that a moth flies into your eye, a bird flaps in your face, you get a terrible bout of food poisoning after eating seafood or you are bitten by a dog when you're a child. Trauma can also be induced by someone else's reaction: for example, you might have been really young when you saw your mother fly into a panic over a huge spider. Because you saw her panic, you panicked – and so that one, intense event left you with a phobia of spiders.

Phobia caused by conditioning

A phobia can also develop over time through conditioning. To use the example of spiders again, a phobia may start because you see that your parents are scared of spiders *or* you may quite arbitrarily decide you don't like them. You then tell yourself that you really don't like them and start to avoid them. You become hypersensitive to spiders and are constantly on the lookout for them – and so the phobia starts to develop and become more ingrained.

Conditioning by association can also happen when something that you're slightly uncomfortable with begins to cause you anxiety. For example, let's say you feel a bit nervous about driving but you still drive as usual. Then one day you panic when you're turning right and, because you already have a slight dislike of driving, this becomes your phobia because you believe you're more likely to be in an accident if you turn right.

Case Study

Isabella was phobic of snakes. Snakes are something that most of us feel a bit uncomfortable about, and if we saw one in our garden we wouldn't rush up to it for a cuddle. But we know that snakes don't hang out in our back gardens or wander down the street, and so our discomfort, or even fear, remains contained. Isabella, however, was convinced that snakes wanted to kill her and that they wanted to do this so much that they would find a way into her home, no matter what.

She had never actually been up close to a snake so she hadn't developed her phobia through trauma; instead she had developed her fear through conditioning and avoidance. Isabella had seen snakes in a zoo when she was a child and her school had organized for a snake handler to come to one of their school assemblies. While she hadn't particularly enjoyed either experience, she had no real reason to be petrified. Isabella just told herself that she didn't like snakes and that she was afraid of them. Eventually the phobia got so pronounced that she could be within four miles of a zoo but, because she was convinced they were out to get her, she would ring up the zoo to see if a snake had escaped. She then became afraid of worms because they were slithery and looked similar to snakes.

When you start to avoid something you begin to condition your phobia: you tell yourself you have to avoid it in order to stay safe and you tell yourself this over and over again until you're completely phobic. How extreme your avoidance behaviour is categorizes how extreme your phobia is, so you may avoid certain places or situations or, at the more severe end, you may not even be able to step outside your house.

Phobia as a result of a projected fear

This comes about when somebody cannot think about or accept something painful that is going on in their life, so they end up channelling all of their mental energy into being afraid of something more acceptable and tangible.

Case Study

I worked with a woman called Diane who was terrified of mice and rats. Diane was completely obsessed by this fear because she'd read that there were mice and rats everywhere in London, which was where she lived. She would scan outside her front door before leaving; she wouldn't travel on the tube; she wouldn't go into any parks; she couldn't go anywhere near water; and she wouldn't walk near manhole covers. Diane avoided any situation where there might be mice or rats and so, for much of the time, she stayed indoors.

Through our sessions I learned that Diane's phobia had started in her childhood. Her parents had resented her being born because they'd not felt they could afford to have another child. They didn't hide their resentment and abused her emotionally and neglected her because they blamed her for the way their lives had ended up. Diane was also physically abused by her siblings because she was much younger; they also continually told her she had been an 'accident'.

Although she hated her family, Diane's infant psyche couldn't admit or verbalize this, so she'd channelled her hatred into an acceptable fear – the fear of mice and rats.

HOW DO YOU MAINTAIN A PHOBIA?

Once you have a phobia there are several ways in which you can maintain the fear. All of these are to do with how you allow the phobic object to rule your life.

Avoidance

Phobics believe that as long as they are avoiding their fear, on some level they are winning. Every time they do something to keep successfully out of the way of what they see as potential danger, they reward themselves that they have triumphed. *I'm beating it. I'm winning. It can't get me.*

If you have a phobia, although avoiding your fear may make you feel positive and victorious, if only for a moment, all you are doing is embedding it. Rather than acknowledging that there is no actual danger, you give the message to your brain that it has something to be afraid of – and you cannot get over your phobia until you admit that there really is nothing to avoid.

Critical Self-talk

All phobics criticize themselves for acting irrationally: they know that in reality they can behave differently but, because they don't, they believe they *must* be a bad person. The knock-on effect is that they then believe that the phobic object is coming after them because they deserve to be harmed – and so phobics' critical self-talk focuses on how silly they are and how guilty and embarrassed they feel.

Case Study

To return to Isabella's story, as her phobia got stronger Isabella moved with her family into a flat because she was so afraid of garden worms. She also avoided going to the park with her children; when it came to booking holidays, they had to go on city breaks to avoid beaches and the countryside. Isabella knew that city breaks weren't ideal for her kids but she didn't feel like she had a choice.

While some phobics cling on to their fear because they think it makes them stand out as interesting or attractive, Isabella didn't. She didn't see her phobia as her USP and she knew it didn't make her cute or interesting. She actually really disliked herself for it and knew that her behaviours – like moving house, avoiding the park and not giving her children suitable holidays – were ridiculous, but by giving herself a hard time she gave the phobia more weight and importance in her life. And so it grew and grew.

Isabella felt foolish and guilty for avoiding beautiful holiday destinations, and she was embarrassed by the fact that she wouldn't even go for a walk in the countryside in case she came across an adder. She also worried about how silly she would feel if she ever had to admit that there was no need to be afraid. Her thought process went something like this: *What if it's not true? What if my fear is irrational and unfounded? I've been phobic for so long that if I prove it's not real and find evidence that there is no reason to be afraid of snakes, what will that say about me? There must be something wrong with me.* Isabella therefore maintained her phobia to justify her actions.

Lack of self-esteem and self-trust

Phobics believe that if they come face to face with their phobic objects they won't be able to cope, and that they therefore can't trust themselves to keep themselves safe. They say to themselves, *I won't be able to cope. I'll freak out. I'll lose control. I'll make a fool of myself. I'll be even more vulnerable.* By not believing in themselves enough to know that they can deal with whatever they have to face, and by not trusting themselves to keep safe and protected, phobics build up lots of reasons to stay afraid.

The power of imagination

Another way that phobics can maintain their fear is through their imagination. Phobics have strong and creative imaginations. Phobics can see the most horrible things happening to them, and so they feel threatened and live in dread of what the future holds. They are able to conjure up, with very little effort, the worst-possible scenario. If they do this hundreds of times over a number of years, their brain begins to believe their imaginings. Their thoughts become a prediction rather than an illusion, and because they can see it clearly, they believe it *will* happen.

Even if we're not phobic, most of us can relate to this kind of self-fulfilling thinking. For example, imagine that you are convinced that your partner will leave you. (If you're not in a relationship, see if you can think of someone else you know who has done this.) By the time you've imagined it over and over again, you start to believe that they really will leave you.

Your imagination is incredibly powerful but, as you will see later in this chapter, when you use it to your advantage it can play a vital role in overcoming your phobia.

The need for denial

We're all able to deny and ignore things in our lives, but if something very traumatic happens to you and you want to block it completely out of your mind, the emotions related to that event will surface somewhere else. For example, if you want to forget that your parents were abusive or emotionally absent, you will replace those traumatic memories with emotions that are as strong as the emotions around the abuse: a slight fear or worry won't be enough to numb the pain so you replace it with an extremely intense phobia. You will remember this happening in Diane's case earlier in this chapter where she used her phobia of mice and rats to block out her hatred of her family. Here is another, very different, case study.

Case Study

Hannah came to me for therapy two years after her husband of eight years had suddenly died. Understandably she was devastated, but two years on her grief was still unbearable to the point where she genuinely believed that her grief would kill her. Hannah was so convinced that her grief would kill her and had become so paranoid of getting ill that she became phobic of germs.

Hannah was in denial about how lonely and sad she was, and these emotions were replaced by her phobia and her obsessive need to clean. She thought she was avoiding friends because she didn't want to catch any germs, but unconsciously what was going on was that Hannah thought that her friends' sympathy was running out, so she used her phobia of getting ill to retreat from them. She also believed she was staying indoors to reduce her chances of coming across germs – but she was really hiding away from the rest of the world because her feelings of loss were so overwhelming. This was understandable as this very real and powerful loss is completely devastating.

Before I could even start treating Hannah we had to deal with her fears about the germs she'd face on her journey to my clinic and when she got here. Once we overcame these hurdles, her therapy process was about acknowledging her grief and her own fear of dying. As we did this, the phobia itself lessened, so once we came to deal with the phobia directly, it was a much simpler process.

HOW TO TREAT PHOBIAS

Relaxation and anxiety are incompatible responses: you literally cannot experience phobic and calm responses at the same time. This is the crux of the recovery treatment for phobias. If you learn to associate a feeling of calm with your phobia, you will find that you can't feel petrified about it. You disconnect the fear from the object causing the fear and, as a result, you no longer feel phobic.

It's essential that you realize you can face your fear and keep control. If you have had your phobia for a long time, you will have spent much of your life feeling as if your fear is a dark mess that you carry around with you. The treatment process is designed to change the way you see your fear. It will help you turn and face your dark mess and you will see that it's not as messy or dark as you thought.

In psychology we call this process 'desensitization' – but before you go through this process for real you need to do it in your imagination first. Once you are confident that you can face your phobic object in your head, you can do it for real.

Having a phobia is terrifying and the process of getting rid of it can be frightening too if it's not done in an ethical and caring way. That's why we do this treatment in stages. You will see that you can do certain parts of this process on your own, but that in some parts you will need a partner. This can be a professional, such as a counsellor, psychologist or psychotherapist, or it can be a trusted close friend.

Visual Desensitization

Visual desensitization is the process of imagining your phobic object and learning to be calm and controlled at the thought of it. You learn to broach your fear in a manageable way without panicking, freaking out or feeling unnecessarily afraid. You start with a mildly phobic object and then work up to more frightening things until you can imagine coping with your biggest fear. To make this process even more comfortable, each visualization is alternated with a relaxing visualization exercise.

Visualization desensitization also starts to eliminate the effects of anticipatory anxiety. Anticipatory anxiety is when you catastrophize the situation to such a point that rather than thinking, *If I see a snake it will slither past me,* you think, *If I see a snake it will slither right up to me, crawl around my neck, attack me and kill me.* To overcome this you have to bring the fear into a more rational arena. Over time, you can get a permanent hold on this rational way of thinking.

Now that you understand what you are going to do, here is the process. To illustrate it clearly I will take you through each step I used with Isabella and her phobia of slithery things. This will give you a good idea of what you need to do to overcome your phobia or to help someone else overcome theirs.

1 Visualize Your Safe Haven

Start by visualizing a place where you feel calm and safe, while you are actually in a calm, safe place. Don't try this at work or while travelling but when you are curled up safe and warm at home. This could be your living room or your bedroom or your garden – wherever you feel most comfortable and protected. If you don't have a place where you feel safe, imagine one that you would like to have and make it as clear an image as if it really existed. Picture your safe haven and, if you're working with someone, describe to your partner what this place looks like in as much detail as possible.

By using your imagination you will invoke all the feelings you have when you're in that place. This will act as your safe haven throughout the process: it will be the place that you return to in your mind whenever you start to feel anxious or afraid.

For Isabella, her safe place was her living room, so I got her to describe her living room to me in such vivid detail that not only she but I too felt as if we were there.

2 Visualize Your Mild Phobic Object

Once you have somewhere to retreat if you start to feel frightened, the next step is to imagine your phobic object in a mild form. I don't want you to immediately think about the most petrifying thing you can: this is just a small step. If you're afraid of dogs, you might think of a Snoopy or another cartoon-character dog. The idea is for you to dip your toe in the water – not for you to dive in.

Isabella imagined a cartoon worm, because while worms were something she was phobic about, cartoons were towards the bottom of her phobic scale.

3 Alternate with the Visualization of Your Safe Haven

After visualizing your mild phobic object, think back to your safe haven. This should reverse any signs of fear you were starting to feel and begins the process of disconnecting your fear. Once you are back in a controlled state and feel safe and strong, go back to visualizing your mild phobic object, then continue alternating the two images until you feel neutral about the mild phobic object. Don't worry about how long this takes – hours, days, weeks or months – slowly but surely is effective.

4 Repeat with a More Frightening Object

Once you've proved that you can keep calm while picturing something you're phobic about, take this a bit further and think of something slightly more frightening – something that would usually make your phobic response stronger. For this step, Isabella imagined a real worm.

As before, whenever you start to feel afraid, take yourself back to your safe haven. Make yourself think about being calm and protected. It's also important at this stage that you stop giving your phobic object any intent; this is where it can really help to work with another person. If you start to think about what your phobic object is going to do to you, your partner or the professional you are working with has to step in and interrupt that thought by encouraging you to think rationally.

For example, when Isabella started to say, *The snake's thinking about hurting me,* I would interrupt her and say, *Can snakes really think maliciously?* Or if she said, *The snake's coming to attack me,* I'd challenge her by saying, *Is that really true? Is the snake not more afraid of you than you are of it?*

After alternating the visualizations a few times and rationalizing the anxious thoughts, you should be able to imagine being near this phobic object without being scared.

5 Repeat with an Even More Frightening Object

You finish the exercise by repeating this process for all the things that make up your phobia and, as always, remember to use your safe haven to keep you in a calm state.

Isabella did this step by visualizing small snakes. She then imagined being at a zoo with her kids and taking them up to the snake tank.

This process of visual desensitization is critical to the treatment of phobias, and works because it chips away at the phobia in three ways:

1. It introduces the process of rational thinking
2. It teaches you how to feel calm and safe at any time
3. It instils a sense of self-belief because you begin to see that you can cope.

Real-life Desensitization

Real-life desensitization works on the same principles as visual desensitization in that it involves systematic exposure to your phobic object. It also works on a similar hierarchy system, starting with the easiest object right up to what you're most phobic about.

When done with care and in a totally supportive environment, this process is very valuable and powerful. You don't have to be in therapy but you do need a supportive, helpful partner if you want to work through the complete process. You also have to remember that, as the phobic, *you* control when you move on to the next level. It's always done in your own time. Because you will actually be dealing with the real phobic objects, it's essential that you get the hierarchy right, so you must map this out before you do anything else.

1 Create Your Phobic Hierarchy (Bourne, 1998)

You need to list 10 different phobic objects and number them 1–10, with 1 as the least frightening and 10 as the most frightening. If you can't come up with 10 things, think again – almost all phobics have lots of feared and anticipated events that appear real to them.

Also decide on a fear rating for each one so that you know you have them in the right order.

Here's Isabella's hierarchy:

Order	Phobic object	Fear Rating
1	Snakeskin shoes	4
2	Feather boa	5
3	Worm	6
4	Two worms	7
5	Small British snake far away in a field	7
6	2–3-inch British adder 1 metre away	9
7	2–3-inch British adder in the same field as me and I can't get out	9
8	Lots of snakes	10
9	Seeing big snake when on holiday abroad	10
10	Being close enough to a python that it could attack	10

2 Work Out Why Each Item Is Frightening

Once you have your top-10 phobic items and you've worked out their fear rating, you need to start the process of understanding the fear. This helps you know the underlying reasons for your phobia and therefore exactly what you have to be exposed to in order to overcome it. So for each item on the list, ask yourself or get your partner to ask you:

What's particularly scary about that?

To the non-phobic and, when in a rational frame of mind, to the phobic themselves, these answers will not necessarily make sense; but for the phobia to exist there has to be the tiniest possibility in the phobic's mind that they are true.

Here are some of Isabella's answers to why her phobic objects made her feel afraid and insecure:

Snakeskin shoes: *these were once part of a snake so the intention to hurt me might still be there. If I wear them they might make me walk under a train.*

Feather boa: *this is the same 'boa' as in boa constrictor so there could be a connection to snakes.*

Worms: *worms might be friends with snakes. The snakes might have told the worms to follow me. The worms might then curl around my big toe and make it fall off.*

Small British snake in field far away: *it might shoot across to get me.*

Several snakes: *this would be like an army of snakes so they could attack me in a strategic way.*

Seeing a big snake when on holiday abroad: *foreign snakes are poisonous and can kill so I'm sure they'll kill me.*

Pythons: *pythons can kill. I've seen them in films so I know how dangerous they are and I'm sure they'll come to get me.*

Underlying all of these things was Isabella's belief that snakes hated her and wanted to kill her. Again Isabella knew this was unlikely and to anyone else it really did seem ridiculous; but she couldn't say that it was totally impossible. If there was any chance of these things happening, even a tiny seed of possibility, her fear would latch on to it and confirm her phobia.

You often see a similar process of superstitious magical thinking in the way children see ghosts. They might not believe in ghosts but they say they do because they think that if they say they don't, the ghosts will come to get them just to prove they exist. This is where the parallel lies with phobias: if Isabella stopped saying she was afraid of snakeskin shoes or worms or snakes, she believed they would come to get her just to prove she was wrong.

3 Challenge the Negative Self-talk

The next thing to do once you have a complete hierarchy and understanding of why each object is frightening is to delve deeper into the things your critical voice says and to start challenging these self-criticisms. By doing this you will build up your confidence and be able to talk back to your negative voice. The way to do this is to make two lists of mantras of positive statements: one that undermines your phobic beliefs and one that builds your self-esteem.

First of all, create some statements that directly negate your beliefs about your phobic object. For Isabella these were:

Snakes wish me no harm.
Snakes are more afraid of me than I am of them.
The snakes do not single me out.
Snakes are not out to get me.

Second you build your self-confidence by realizing you are a good person and don't deserve to be harmed. The way to do this is to list 10 compliments that you can tell yourself every day to challenge your self-doubt. As with sufferers of anxiety, it may be hard to do this because you're more used to putting yourself down than building yourself up, but with enough time you will be able to find 10 things about you that you like and appreciate.

With two sets of mantras at your fingertips, you can use these foundations to prepare for the real-life exposure. Just be aware that this step may reveal some underlying reasons why the phobia exists.

In Isabella's case her low self-esteem and critical talk were both linked to the biblical connotation of the serpent in the Garden of Eden. She thought that because she was a bad person, the snakes had picked her out to punish her. She thought she mustn't be a good person if she couldn't even trust herself to cope with the idea of facing a snake, and even though we had started to challenge this by showing her she could cope with the visual systematic desensitization, there was still a lot of work to do.

4 Begin the Real-life Exposure

In the same way that you used your calm space for the visual desensitization, you need to have that tool at your fingertips for this next stage so that any time you start to feel your fear taking over, you can control your response. If you haven't already found someone to work with, you will need the help of either a professional or a supportive friend to work further in the process. If you are struggling to find someone you can ask your GP or contact the National Phobics Society. Whomever you choose and however you find them, make sure this person allows you to keep control of the process and that they are committed to work with you until you have finished all the steps.

Start by imagining your safe haven. Once you feel centred and in control, get your partner/therapist to bring the first object on your hierarchy into the room. Get as close to it as you feel comfortable doing and have a good look at it, taking in as much detail as you can. If you start to feel your fear response kick in, move away from the object and return to your imagined safe haven.

Isabella did this first step with a pair of snakeskin shoes. She took them out of the box and looked at them and then went back to her safe haven. In the same session, she put on one of the shoes – and then returned to her safe haven. She also repeated her mantras to reinforce the fact she was actually successfully confronting her phobia and by breathing and overriding her critical voice, Isabella stopped her body from responding to her fear. At the end of the session, she managed to put on both shoes and walk around in them. She used mantras to keep control of herself. *I'm in control of these shoes. They are harmless. They are inanimate. They have no intent to harm me.*

This first step in the real-life desensitization process is a breakthrough point. If you have been terrified of something for many years, maybe even most of your life, you will be thrilled that you've interacted with that object without freaking out. It will make you realize you're in control because you're standing and facing your fear.

5 Repeat Step 4 for Every Item on Your Hierarchy

Do not expect to work all the way up your hierarchy in one session! The safest way to do this will be to do one stage at a time so that you have time to fully integrate your progress. I suggest you keep up the momentum on your progress by leaving no more than one full day in between each stage and, if you have a day in between stages, spend these days repeating your mantras so that you cement the strong foundation you've built.

Here are all the stages that Isabella went through:

Session 2: Isabella put a feather boa around her neck and she then returned to her safe haven. She then put the boa back on while repeating her mantras.

Session 3: I brought into the consulting room a worm in a closed see-through box: there was no way it could get out. Isabella looked at it and then returned to her calm space.

I then took the worm out of the box and put it on my hand, and then Isabella put the worm on her own hand. On the same day we also managed to go through this same process with two worms – with Isabella returning to her safe haven as usual.

Session 4: We had a two-foot snake in a glass box on the far side of the consulting room: there was no way it could get out. This was the closest we could get to Isabella's fear of a snake being in a field and it invoked the same level of fear. Isabella could see that the snake was scared of her and wanted to stay in its box. She learned that British snakes don't want to be near to humans and by learning this Isabella was able to build a rational argument why not to be afraid of snakes. At the end of the session, I stood two metres away from Isabella, took the snake out and held it. This sent her fear rating up to 8 so she returned to her safe haven and we called it a day.

Note on using animals: Whenever I used real snakes there was a snake handler present. It's vitally important that, when using animals, you have an expert present. You should never frighten the animals you're using – whether they're wild birds, domestic pets, snakes or spiders; and we're very lucky that there are professionals who are willing to help people overcome their fear while protecting the animals as well.

Session 5: On this day we did exactly what we'd done in session 4 so as not to move too quickly and overwhelm Isabella.

It's important to mention here that you must remember to complete this process in your own time. It's critical that you avoid flooding. This means being exposed to too much too quickly, as this can trigger the phobic response and undo the work done so far.

Session 6: Building on the last two sessions, I managed to stand one metre away from Isabella while holding the snake, and she gradually moved towards me until she was next to me. For Isabella to think rationally, she needed to realize that the snake wasn't after me or her and that it also didn't differentiate between us. It wasn't the Garden of Eden and she wasn't being judged. Isabella was proud of herself at the end of the session because she could see that she was really starting to overcome her phobia. Her pride also became self-complimentary and she began to self-validate and like herself a bit more.

Sessions 7 & 8: We used three snakes in these sessions and we had a couple of snake handlers present. We followed the same process as before, getting Isabella to move nearer to the snakes when she felt comfortable. We also kept going over the rational thought process because I had to be sure that Isabella had practised this enough that she could rely on it to take over immediately whenever she needed it.

Session 9: Two five-foot snakes were at the other end of the room and in this session Isabella wasn't comfortable with them moving any nearer to her at all – but she did keep control of her breathing and her state.

Session 10: We managed to get the two five-foot snakes two metres away from Isabella, which was entirely appropriate. She was feeling rational and it was important for her expectations to be managed. There was no need for Isabella to be any closer to overcome her phobia because unless she was going to work with snakes (which was definitely out of the question) she would never need to be any nearer. She said she couldn't touch them but that was fine: all you have to do to overcome your phobia is what you would have to do in day-to-day life. She didn't need to hold or touch a snake – she simply needed to see that snakes had no malicious intent and that they didn't see her as any different to anyone else. What Isabella needed to know was that she could get close enough to have a look, which meant she could go on safari and enjoy the experience.

Session 11: We finally made it to the python, by which point Isabella was determined to finish the process. As we've said before, one of the key things is for the phobic to think rationally, so in the case of the python it would be wrong for Isabella to think it was harmless: pythons are not harmless animals but while one might try to attack her because by its very nature it's a dangerous animal, it would not be out to get her specifically because she was a bad person. This brought Isabella's fear into a rational arena because this is what other people would think.

Isabella did actually manage to touch the python, which was more than she ever dreamt she'd be able to do. She had done more than enough to beat her phobia and was extremely proud of herself. She had replaced her negative self-talk with a complimentary voice; she had achieved her goal; and she had done unbelievably well.

To get to the last items on the hierarchy we needed a handler present. Even with the knowledge that pythons aren't venomous, I wasn't too keen on having two five-foot snakes or a python in my consulting room. My heart quickened and I had to control my own natural fear response. You have to remember that at the top end of a phobic hierarchy you may be dealing with things that even a non-phobic would be scared of. Poisonous or not, large snakes can be terrifying for someone who's never had a phobia but most people wouldn't put themselves in a position to find out how frightening they are. Phobics deserve full respect for facing their fears in this way. I can tell you, it's not pleasant coming face to face with a python!

The key things to reiterate in this process are: remember not to flood; go slowly, calmly and safely; keep breathing; use your safe haven whenever you need; and take as much time as you need. Finally, realize how far you want to go and what you have to face to be able to live your life without fear.

Note on Overcoming All Phobias

There can be come mildly negative consequences of curing a phobia, particularly if it is a projected fear. After you engage with your fear, realize you don't need to deny it any longer and let it go, you may experience a moment of euphoria. You will suddenly realize you can live life freely – but then you may experience regret; so freedom can come with the negative consequence of self-criticism.

Case Study

When Isabella started to regain her freedom, rather than just enjoy life, she focused on all the time she had wasted trapped inside her house. She started to think she was stupid and pathetic and so she held back from living her life to the full. Even though Isabella went on holiday, she didn't relax. When she went to the park and saw how much pleasure such a simple thing could give, she became very sad. When she went shopping in town, she got angry with herself for having not done something so easy before and her criticism of having had the phobia at all overshadowed her joy at having beaten it.

Once you begin to go out and enjoy life again, as Isabella did, you might realize how much time you wasted and how much of life you missed by clinging on to your fear for so long, and you may give yourself a hard time about it and wonder why you didn't deal with it earlier. If you let this regret grow, criticize yourself for it and torment yourself with what you've missed out on, you can end up bullying yourself and retreating from the world again. This is similar to the way in which a healthy level of insecurity, if left to grow, can become social anxiety.

You have to avoid being critical. Stop at the first sign of self-criticism and say: *That is not the point*. Forgive yourself for having the phobia because you now understand why you had it, and simply be pleased about having beaten it. Rather than focus on the regret of not having faced your fear sooner, you need to engage with the success of overcoming your fear – and in this way you can keep moving forward in life and not backwards. Praise yourself for not turning your prison sentence into a life sentence and give yourself credit for facing your fear at all.

TAKE-HOME TIPS

If you feel inspired to overcome your phobias, here are some things you can do straight away:

1 Challenge your negative self-talk

Make a list of positive statements that undermine your phobic beliefs and a list of 10 compliments about yourself. These don't have to be related to your phobia. Say these every day – whether you believe them or not.

2 Create your safe haven

Visualize the place where you feel most calm and safe. Breathe slowly through your nose with your shoulders relaxed and, if you wish to, use the Home Position. Remember that this is a critical step. You may only be creating this in your imagination but it's vital that you have this space set up as your comfort zone.

3 Face the cause of your phobia

If you think your phobia may be a projected fear – if you can't think when it started or why it might have become a phobia and you have had a traumatic experience or relationship that started before the phobia – you can spend some time working out whether you have a projected fear.

While you will need professional help with curing this, you can have a go now at writing out all the things you'd rather not think about. To give you a clear idea of what I mean, let's look back at Diane's projected phobia of mice and rats.

Case Study

The list of things Diane didn't want to think about looked like this:

My mum
Childhood memories of holidays
I never got any birthday presents or had birthday parties
Feeling unloved and unlovable
The times my mum hit me
My mum saying I was an accident
My mum favouring my brothers and sisters
My parents telling me about the sacrifices they had to make because I was born

I then asked Diane the following questions: were any of these things her fault? Was it her fault that she was born? Was she to blame for her mother hitting her – or was it just her mother's parenting style? Was it Diane's fault that her birthdays weren't celebrated? When I asked Diane to look at each of these things rationally she could see that none of these happened because of anything she had done: she was an innocent child.

You may feel as if you have an overwhelming mess following you around but once you start to look into this you will realize it's not as frightening as you may think.

This list will form the basis of your recovery and will help with any therapy process.

If you find it hard to stand back from your list, imagine you're talking to someone else. Would you tell one of your friends that they were to blame for being hit or that it was their fault that they were emotionally abused? By stepping back you may find it easier to think logically rather than emotionally.

Then you have to ask yourself, if these things were not your fault, can they really destroy you? Can the memory still hurt you? Do you have to hide these memories behind your phobia? If you've felt pain through the original events and then even more pain through your phobia, is it not time to acknowledge these memories were not your fault and accept that they don't have to hurt you any more?

As an adult you are much safer than you were as a child so you can free yourself from all of your fears and traumas and compensate for these traumas by caring for yourself now. When you realize that you don't need your phobia any more and you start to engage with your memories and deal with them, you can free yourself of two fears – fear of your past and the fear you currently experience through your phobia.

ONE FINAL THOUGHT ...

It's ironic that you may be petrified of something yet spend all your time thinking about it; but the good news is that you no longer have to be haunted by your phobia: you now have the skills to beat it. By working through this process you can become free of a phobia of any object. The process is logical and designed to keep you safe and in control. Your phobia may have been holding you back and dominating you for many years but you can choose to get rid of it at any time and experience what it's like to be in charge of your own life.

CHAPTER 11

PHOBIAS OF STATES

Take a minute to imagine that you're having a really bad day. People are being nasty to you, everyone seems to be judging you and you feel uncomfortable in your own skin. You feel so stressed and upset that as soon as you get home all you want to do is go to bed. You crawl under your duvet with a hot cup of tea or a big glass of wine and you pretend the rest of the world isn't there. When you're safely tucked in your bed you start to feel OK: you feel cosy and protected and you want to stay like that for ever.

I'm sure most of you have had a similar experience – a time when you wanted to feel safe and cocooned. I asked you to imagine this because this experience of wanting to hide from the world is a momentary glimpse at agoraphobia: although agoraphobia is a relentless need to hide, I want you to realize that there is no reason to stigmatize phobias, because many of them stem from common human emotions and I hope that by relating to this situation, even if you don't suffer yourself, you can start to understand this kind of fear.

Living with a phobia is like living trapped in your own head and although you don't have to confront your phobic situation or object all the time, you *think* about it continuously. Not only are you haunted by the thought of your phobic object but you are also gripped by the physical aspect of it. At any time, you may find your palms go clammy, your legs might go weak, you can get a ringing in your ears, you may feel hot and sweaty and your heart may start racing. Your fear affects you physically and mentally because you are constantly preoccupied by your phobic state. You can't enjoy anything you're doing because you're constantly worried that you'll come across your phobic object: it's as if your present and what may be your future fold together.

The difference between a fear and a phobia, which as I described in the last chapter about phobias of objects also applies to phobias of states. For example, a person who is *afraid* of heights and a person who is *phobic* of heights will both react in the same way when they're actually in a tall building but the difference is clear when they think about being in a tall building. Someone who is afraid won't like the thought of being in a tall building but they won't be gripped mentally and physically by their terror, whereas a phobic person will react in the same way and with the same intensity merely at the thought of being in a tall building. So, as you can see, phobias are a very intense and relentless form of fear.

Case Study

One of my clients, Susie, had a fear of heights. She worried that if she was in a high place she would throw herself off. This phobia was connected to a deep sense of self-doubt and stemmed from the fact that Susie had been clumsy as a child. When she thought about tripping up she didn't trust herself to stay on her feet. She didn't have suicidal tendencies, her fear simply came from the evidence of being awkward when she was growing up. This memory of being uncoordinated developed into the belief, *I might trip over and fall off.* This became, *Heights are unsafe, so I might trip over and fall off,* which developed into, *I'm unsafe on heights, so I might throw myself off,* which escalated into, *If I go anywhere near a high building I might be tempted to throw myself off.*

As a result Susie was too scared to even walk past a tall building. When she did have to she didn't trust herself to keep safe and imagined in vivid detail what it would be like to throw herself off. Because of this, she conditioned her brain so that every time she saw a tall building, she felt deep mistrust for herself. Lack of trust in yourself leads to fear because you don't believe you're able to keep yourself safe and so that's how Susie developed her fear of heights.

As you can see from Susie's story, phobias can counteract your personality. It doesn't matter how bubbly and outgoing you are; when faced with your phobia, you become anxious and out of control, a state which may be completely different from your natural personality. This is when fear can become a fundamentally disabling psychological disorder.

In the previous chapter I covered the different causes of phobias and other general information on phobias of objects; so in this chapter I will focus on giving you a deep understanding of the most common phobias of situations – agoraphobia and claustrophobia. I hope that, by doing this, I can show you how ordinary rational people, like you and me, can grow to be so afraid of what's around them that their whole life gets turned upside down.

AGORAPHOBIA

While most of us feel from time to time that the world is too much to bear, agoraphobics feel that the world is *always* too much to bear. They don't have the odd day when they feel like they want to hide from the world – they feel like that every day. They think they're continually being judged and criticized by other people because they can't cope and they believe that beyond their front door lurks a world full of danger. They feel so overwhelmed and obsessed by this that they can't even bear to leave their house.

This phobia of open spaces and the outside world can be found in two forms. In some cases agoraphobics have actually experienced a dangerous situation, which either ended in them or someone else being hurt: for example, they might have been raped or mugged or they could have been the victim of an attempted murder. In cases like this it's completely appropriate and understandable that their natural response is to hide and protect themselves. Most people would react in this way if something like this happened to them; but in most cases when people hide, they go through a recovery period and then return to life as it was before. With agoraphobics, however, they don't recover. They don't regain the confidence to venture outside. Their fear grows and grows until they never want to go out again.

The other kind of agoraphobia starts when people are paranoid about being judged. Again, most of us can relate to this because we all experience it to some degree. If you've ever broken the heel on your shoe, you know how it feels to be terribly self-conscious as you hobble along, hoping nobody will notice. Or if you've ever been out and suddenly realized that your shirt has a big hole in it and everyone has seen it, you just want to get home as quickly as possible. If you've ever been in a situation like this you will understand how it feels to be embarrassed, uncomfortable and under scrutiny, so you can empathize to some degree – but this is how agoraphobics feel all of the time. They feel that they're being looked at and judged every time they go out and they intensify these feelings of discomfort to such a degree that they believe they can't cope with anything – and so they stay indoors where they feel safe. But being a prisoner in your own home is no way to live.

Case Study

One of my clients, Jill, had both kinds of agoraphobia. She had witnessed someone being mugged and consequently formed the belief that the world was dangerous. She stayed at home while she was getting over the trauma but during this recovery period she started to obsess about how everyone was, as she called it, a 'victim-in-waiting' and she came to the conclusion that if she stepped out of her house, she would definitely be mugged. Jill was convinced that everyone would see she was weak and not good enough to cope, and so would target her.

She also created another belief: that she was vulnerable and fragile and 'too pathetic' to deal with the outside world. She used to say to herself: I'm not good enough. I'll be attacked because I'm pathetic, and the more she said these things, the more the two sides of her agoraphobia came together. Over a period of time, Jill's fear grew into a totally debilitating phobia.

In the beginning it was very tricky to treat Jill because she wouldn't leave the house to come to my clinic. While it is possible to work with someone over the phone, I choose not to do this because face-to-face I feel I can offer full support to my client as they work through what can be very painful issues. This could mean going to someone's house but I don't ever do this either because I don't want to raise their vulnerabilities and discuss their fears in the one place where they feel safe. I don't want to leave negative feelings in their home and so I always have to get my clients to my clinic; I do this using systematic desensitization. When I'm in my treatment room I can offer my clients the appropriate support and set the right boundaries and frame to deal with their fear.

So, in Jill's case, because she had a lot of unconscious and involuntary physical reactions to her fear, I started by helping her control the physical symptoms. Even before she left her house Jill had worked on her breathing and her mantras. We then divided up the route between her house and my treatment room. She made each step of the journey in sequence with a close friend whom she trusted implicitly, and we even booked the same taxi driver each week to make Jill feel as comfortable as possible. It took five weeks for Jill to be able to do the whole journey, but she got there in the end.

Once Jill had made it to my clinic, initially I made sure that she never had to wait in the waiting room but could come straight into my therapy room. I also made sure that there was a doctor on standby, because Jill was convinced she was going to faint. The reason I did all of these things was because I didn't want to flood Jill with her fear. Jill could of course get to my clinic without passing out, but she wasn't ready yet to accept the reality of her fear and so we had this plan in place for every visit she made.

I then spent the first session working on her feelings of inadequacy and fragility because for the therapy to work it was essential that she felt comfortable in my room and that she didn't feel she was being judged in any way. I also gave Jill what's known as psychoeducation: I taught her about what she was experiencing so that, as well as making emotional and practical changes, she could start to get a rational hold over her phobia. I wanted Jill to see the logic that although she had seen someone being mugged and while there are dangers in the world, she wouldn't be targeted every time she stepped outside her front door.

Jill needed to get to a point where she acknowledged the potential risk but only in so much as it affects everyone: Jill had to stop believing that she would be singled out for attack.

We also had to go through a systematic desensitization; but because agoraphobics are afraid of everything outside their front door, we couldn't desensitize each and every object, place and person. After doing a lot of work on building Jill's confidence, I started by doing a visual systematic desensitization and she chose her walled garden as her safe haven.

We worked through the process of imagining what it would be like to travel to my clinic on her own; what it would be like to sit in the waiting room with one person, two people and up to ten people; and then eventually what it would be like to walk along a busy street. In between each of these steps, Jill returned in her mind to the safe haven of her garden and focused on calming down her breathing. We kept a check on her fear symptoms by using a fear rating of 1–10 (with 1 being the least afraid) and no matter how high her fear had gone, we always waited until Jill felt a fear rating of only 2 before we moved on to the next step.

Once we had done this visual process, Jill was ready to start her real-life desensitization. Jill built up to making the journey to my clinic on her own. Then she slowly built up to sitting in the waiting room when there were a couple of people there, then when there were four people, and eventually she was able to wait in a full waiting room.

So not only was the therapy process itself helping Jill break down her phobia but the process of getting used to the journey from home was also empowering her.

We then repeated this process until Jill felt confident walking down a busy street. This whole process took many months but it was worth it: by the end, Jill's self-esteem was at an all-time high and it was no longer a problem for her to face the world.

CLAUSTROPHOBIA

I am going to use this phobia to take you through the detailed recovery process for phobias of states, but first of all I'll introduce you to Bob.

Case Study

Bob suffered from claustrophobia and it was affecting all areas of his life. His friends loved adventure sports but when they went potholing he couldn't go and he also wouldn't get into his daughter's Wendy house to play with her. Bob's fear even went as far as affecting what kind of car he would get into: he wouldn't get into small two-seater cars because he was convinced he'd be trapped. But while Bob was afraid of all enclosed spaces, his fear was focused on lifts, and it was this aspect of his phobia that particularly affected his everyday life. He would walk up 20 flights of stairs to avoid getting in a lift and if he was going away, he would check out the hotel beforehand to see if he could have a room on a lower floor. Bob even had to turn down a job in a bank because the office was on such a high floor in the block that it was only accessible by lift. Bob's fear was affecting his personal life and his career progression, and he had had enough of feeling limited by it – and that's when he came to me for help.

Ω *The Recovery Process for Phobias of States*

To recover fully from a phobia you have to attack the fear from several angles: how the fear manifests in daily life, the underlying issues, and the lack of self-esteem. You have to follow a process to be able to work on these things simultaneously and I want to show you how this works through Bob's journey.

I Find the underlying issue

To someone who doesn't suffer from one of these phobias, it might seem pretty straightforward that you would work to eliminate the fear of the phobic state, in Bob's case the fear of enclosed spaces. However, it's also absolutely essential that you pinpoint the underlying cause of the fear, which is not always evident.

Case Study

As with most phobias of state, although Bob's fear manifested as claustrophobia, there was an underlying issue that had caused it in the first place. During our time together Bob and I worked out that for him this was a fear of getting trapped and losing control.

In talking about control, we covered what it meant to him, what decisions he felt he had no control over and where he could gain control in his life.

All of Bob's issues in this area had stemmed from the fact that his father had been very academic and domineering. He had taken control of all of Bob's major decisions while he was growing up, such as what GCSEs he sat, what A levels he chose, which university he went to and what he studied. In Bob's case his father had made all of the everyday decisions that most people make for themselves. Even when Bob left home when he was 23, his father played a major role in deciding where he lived and even what car he drove.

Although Bob was distanced from his father and free to rule his own life, it was only then that his claustrophobia began to take hold. To most people it would make sense that Bob would now become more confident at this time but the opposite was true: he'd never had to decide for himself and take control of what he did and the prospect terrified him. Bob didn't trust himself to make decisions. He told himself he wasn't good enough and he had become afraid of his own freedom. Rather than deal with this, he channelled his fear into claustrophobia: by being scared of small places he was able to focus his fear without dealing with the real cause. So you can see that Bob's phobia did not stem from a fear of small spaces – it grew out of a fear of life. By pinpointing this fear we knew exactly what we had to get rid of.

2 Create a new internal dialogue

If you want to get over your phobia, you have to work on your internal dialogue. As you can see with all these phobias of states, while the fears are different, they always have a strong element of negative thinking and so it is important to overturn this pattern. As you will have seen in earlier chapters, the best way to do this is to track in a diary what your negative voice is saying. When you write down the harsh critical things you say to yourself, you can realize how cruel that negative voice can be. You know you wouldn't say these kinds of things to someone you loved or cared about – so why should you say them to yourself? You will see me reiterate this over and over again because to overcome any fear, you have to learn to speak to yourself in a kind and gentle way. You have to stop creating a feeling of panic and you have to believe that you are good enough.

The other vital step in creating a new nurturing inner voice is to find five compliments that that negate these criticisms. These can be mantras like *I'm good enough, I'm in control, I can cope,* or things that are personal to you. Phobias are the result of you conditioning yourself to believe that you're not good enough, so you have to condition yourself that you *are* good enough. Before you can break down the phobia itself, you have to rewire the messages inside your brain and train yourself to believe that you are strong, capable and worthy.

Case Study

It was essential for Bob to gain confidence and self-belief that he could cope with the world. Throughout his whole life his father had dominated him and so he never had the chance to see how capable he really was. He had to realize he could make decisions, that he didn't need his father and that he could lead his life on his own terms.

This process had to start with the way Bob spoke to himself. He had to overrule his tendency to undermine himself. By keeping a log of his critical voice, Bob realized that most of the time he said to himself things like: *I'll make the wrong decision. What if I get it wrong? I don't know what to do.* He realized this had to change and so he wrote down a list of positive comments and compliments. The things that worked best for him were: *I can trust myself. I can keep control. I can do it. I am decisive. I am strong.*

Bob read through these mantras every day and this started to recondition his internal dialogue.

3 Visual Desensitization

(Ref: Rothbaum, Hodges, Kooper, Opdyke, Williford, North, 1995).

You will remember from the last chapter on phobias of objects and Jill's earlier case study that the desensitization process starts with a visual process and then moves on to the real-life desensitization (this was developed by Joseph Wolpe in 1958). It's vital that this desensitization is worked through first in the imagination because this lays the foundation for you to be able to cope with facing the actual situation or object; and, as when working with phobias of objects, it's also important that you work through a hierarchy of fear – from the least frightening situations to the most frightening. In Bob's case, I actually worked through the visual and real-life desensitization concurrently.

4 Real-life Desensitization

Case Study

The first step for Bob was to sit in his daughter's Wendy house with the roof off. I wanted him to get used to the enclosed space without being completely surrounded. Once he was able to do this comfortably he sat in it with the roof on.

I then asked Bob to write himself a letter of congratulation. I wanted him to realize what he'd achieved and I got him to write a new letter after each stage in the process. By doing this Bob could see the progress he was making and because he was writing it down, this would act as proof, which we would use later in the process.

The second step was for Bob to crawl inside his daughter's play tunnel and the third was for him to wear a mask. He used a welder's mask and wore it for a while in the safety of his home. By covering his face, the mask symbolized small places.

Bob was now ready to move on to lifts but the first step towards actually going in a lift was to find out about how lifts worked. By becoming familiar with the mechanism and talking to someone who made lifts, Bob began to rationalize that they were safe things that people used and relied on every day and so the grip his fear had on him started to loosen.

Once Bob felt comfortable, he went to an apartment block, stood outside the lift and visualized being in it. He saw himself staying in control and being calm. After this visualization Bob re-read all the letters he'd written to himself about how he'd coped at all the different stages in the process and this helped him cement his belief that not only was he conquering his phobia but he was also fully prepared to actually get in the lift – and that's what he did on the next visit.

Bob went to the same apartment block with a close friend. He chose someone who wasn't critical or judgemental about his phobia and someone whom he trusted implicitly. This friend held the lift doors open while Bob stood inside the lift. After a minute of doing this, he moved back into the corridor and immediately visualized what he'd just done. He also repeated the positive mantras that we'd worked out previously: *I can trust myself. I can keep control. I can do it.* This was a major step for Bob so we left a few days between this and the next critical stage. During this time Bob went back over in his mind each stage he'd done so far and he read his congratulatory letter to remind him.

A few days later Bob went into the lift with his friend and they shut the doors. They stood together for a minute before coming out. Bob spent a few minutes going over this visually in his mind before going in on his own for 10 seconds with the doors shut. He built up to 30 seconds on his own, and that was more than enough for one session. Bob's friend supported and congratulated him and he congratulated himself by writing another letter. By repeating the pattern of success and congratulation, Bob was really starting to see that he could control his fear and he could control himself even when he was in a lift.

A few days later Bob returned to the block and went inside the lift on his own for a minute and by the end of the session he was able to go up and down in the lift for six minutes on his own. He felt fantastic: Bob had conquered his phobia and proved to himself that he was able to lead a balanced life.

But that wasn't the end: to ensure Bob could deal with any event in a lift, I got him to visualize what he would do if the lift broke down. He'd never been stuck in a lift but he could imagine what it would be like and I needed to make sure that he had a strong belief that he would be able to cope, no matter what. Bob watched the episode of *Only Fools and Horses* where Del Boy and Rodney get stuck in a lift and this helped him realize that if you keep calm, everything will be OK because someone will rescue you.

So by the end of our sessions together Bob had worked out the underlying fear of being in control and had worked through a full systematic desensitization. He had also started to conquer the underlying cause by making decisions in his life without feeling afraid or uncomfortable.

Hopefully, you can see from Bob's story that in most cases a phobia of a state is not as straightforward as it looks.

FEAR OF TRAVEL

Phobias are often symbolic, so before I finish this chapter I would like to end by covering the fear of travel, as fears and phobias about travel really indicate very clearly how phobias can be misleading: if you only look at the phobic object and responses, you could miss the point entirely.

Case Study

Angeline had a real fear of travel. It started out as a fear of long journeys because she was afraid of being sick, and then somewhere along the line (although she was unclear as to when) this generalized into not wanting to travel on any public transport. She could drive herself on short journeys as long as she knew the route. If everyone knew where she was she felt safe, but that was the only way she would get about.

On the surface, this looked like a straightforward fear of travel but there was no obvious reason why it had started. Angeline had never been involved in any travel accident or, in fact, had any negative experience when travelling, so I started to ask her what travel meant for her.

Angeline talked about moving on and being committed to that move and I was struck by the language she used. So, using neuro-linguistic programming (created by Bandler and Grinder in 1970) and social constructionist ideas (originated from Durkheim in 1887) – both of which look at how our language constructs our reality – I worked through the words Angeline was using.

Angeline and her partner still lived in the same area where they grew up and she was starting to feel stifled by it. She felt trapped in her life but was in denial about it: she didn't want to be in the same house and in the same town but she couldn't face leaving either. But rather than acknowledge this, she developed her fear of travel so that she didn't have the option of leaving.

To work deeper through this, I helped Angeline focus less on the actual fear of travel and more on what it would be like to be in new places. What transpired was that Angeline was actually afraid of being on her own and when I probed into her relationship she had never discussed these deeper fears with her partner. They had never even contemplated going away on holiday let alone moving house, but when she thought about it

Angeline decided she really did want to move on in her life. So what they did was discuss their new life goals as if Angeline weren't phobic: they took her fear of travel out of the conversation.

What came out of their discussions was that Angeline and her partner did want to make some changes. Luckily her partner didn't feel any particular ties to their home town and they realized that they actually did share goals – but they had never dared to even talk about them.

It took nine months of systematic desensitization to work on this realization: starting with travelling on buses, trains, tubes and ending with Angeline and her partner going on holiday together. Only at that point did Angeline's phobia disappear as well as her fear of being trapped. Angeline had avoided having to think about her freedom by disguising her feeling of being trapped and protecting herself from confronting it through her fear of travel, and now she needed to see that she really did have choices and that she was free.

It can be really useful when treating phobias of state to look behind the fear of the phobic object so that you can discover whether there is another root to the problem that needs dealing with.

TAKE-HOME TIPS

Here are some things you can do straight away:

1. Keep a diary of your negative internal dialogue. Start by doing this for just one hour to get used to the idea.
2. Practise breathing deeply in and out of your nose.
3. Think about what the underlying cause of your fear may be. You may think you have no idea, but just ask yourself the question and see what comes up.
4. Spend five minutes each day visualizing yourself overcoming your fear.

ONE FINAL THOUGHT ...

Phobias of states act as traps and prevent you from living freely. This could be a good thing on the surface, especially if you think your freedom would come at too high a cost. For example, in Angeline's case she thought the price of her freedom would be her relationship. But you need to look at your phobia from all angles to find what it's masking and symbolizing. Seek to focus on yourself and understand yourself and don't be distracted by the nuts and bolts of the phobia itself: explore what lies around it – and through your exploration you'll find out what's really holding you back.

CHAPTER 12

POST TRAUMATIC STRESS DISORDER

You may have heard of 'shell shock' – a condition where war veterans are haunted, often for many years, by memories of the atrocities they had to endure while they were at war. This 'battle fatigue', as it is also known, was prevalent after the two World Wars and has also been seen in more recent times in soldiers who have fought in the Gulf. But you don't have to have been in combat to suffer from this traumatic condition: anyone who has been through a terrifying emotional or physical event can be left with long-term psychological scars. Nowadays this is known as Post Traumatic Stress Disorder.

Post Traumatic Stress Disorder (or PTSD as it is commonly known) is a seriously debilitating condition that comes about as a result of a terrifying physical or emotional event. This could be any traumatic experience such as a rape, attack, accident or even the witnessing of one of these events. The event lives on in your mind as persistent frightening thoughts, memories or flashbacks, and these are so vivid that it can feel as if the event is happening all over again.

There are two reasons this happens: the first is because you cannot assimilate the information caused by the trauma; and the second is that your brain believes that by reliving the event, it's reminding you to watch out for it happening again. It's telling you which situations put you at risk because it knows that you never want to go through that trauma again. But rather than remind you in a calm and gentle way, your brain does this aggressively and relentlessly: you are reminded when you're in the shower, when you're having breakfast, when you're in a meeting and when you're making a cup of coffee. There isn't an external trigger, so the flashbacks can happen at any time, and what's perhaps unconsciously intended to be self-protection becomes self-persecution.

As well as flashbacks, the symptoms of PTSD include panic attacks, being overly jumpy or easily startled, difficulty in sleeping or in falling asleep, lack of confidence, a feeling of having lost control, outbursts of anger, lack of concentration, and hyper-vigilance or being very sensitive to movements and noises. For most of you reading this book, this will be all you need to know about PTSD; but PTSD is a condition that is often misunderstood, so for anyone who does want to know more I have given a very thorough description at the end of the chapter. This is taken from the Diagnostic and Statistical Manual of Mental Disorders 4th edition (DSM-IV) published by the American Psychiatric Association and gives very detailed diagnostic criteria.

As you can see from the symptoms, PTSD affects you on all levels. It can take over your life and stop you from functioning properly at work, at home and at leisure. It can make you feel like a completely different person, as if the traumatic event changed your whole identity. All you can see in yourself is a fearful person: fear becomes your defining factor – the essence of who you are, you feel you have been victimized and become a victim. You stop trusting yourself and it's difficult to believe you can ever get better. The fear that underpins PTSD can be so immense that it alters every aspect of how you think and feel about the world and how you think and feel about yourself.

If you suffer from PTSD or if you're reading this because you want to help someone else who is suffering, it's really important that you believe that it is possible to recover from this condition. The traumatic event may have been controlling your life for a long time but you can learn to take back control. I don't want to overlook what you've been through, because the trauma you experienced was extremely distressing, painful and frightening – but you survived. What happened is in the past and I want to help you move it back there. You can change the way that event affects your life and, although it may not seem like it now, you *can* get your life back on track. I'm going to try to show you that you can regain control of what you do and how you feel and there will come a time when you will be able to do all the things you used to enjoy.

THE FEAR WITHIN PTSD

The fear that comes from a highly traumatic event is so intense that your past and present experiences blur and that's why you experience flashbacks. You can't make a clear distinction in your mind between what happened then and what's happening now. So, for example, you can be making a cup of tea when suddenly you find yourself back in the wreckage of a head-on collision: you see the same things, smell the same smells and feel the terror. It's as if you've been catapulted back in time to that very moment.

Sometimes flashbacks like these are triggered by something that reminds you of the event, but more often than not they happen spontaneously. That's one of the most frightening things about PTSD: you never know when you might get a flashback or have a panic attack. You hold on to the memory at an unconscious level, not because you want to, but because the thought of dealing with it is too overwhelming. You don't think you'll be able to cope and you don't even know where to start. But there is a positive intention in these symptoms: flashbacks are the brain's way of telling you that you haven't finished processing the event.

There are six core fears behind the flashbacks that are particularly prevalent in PTSD. These are taken from Bourne (2000).

1 Fear of loss of control

While you probably don't expect life to be completely predictable, you probably live your life within a basic structure both on a daily level and on a longer-term time scale. You think you know pretty much what will happen to you within the familiar framework of how you live, where you go, what you do at work, what you do outside work and the people you know. There are certain things that you never expect to happen to you – from silly things like being run over by an elephant to more realistic and therefore frightening things like having a car accident or being attacked. Like most people, you assume you'll never have to deal with things like this and, luckily, most of us don't. But there is an element of randomness to life, so when something unexpected does happen, the shock and the after-effects can be devastating.

For a child this could mean a parent leaving you or even dying, because life revolves around your parent or parents and you expect them to always be there. If suddenly one or both of them isn't or aren't, you'll believe that you have no control over your life because, as you see it, you can't even make your parents stay with you. If you're in a serious car accident and you are seriously injured, whether it was your fault or someone else's, you'll feel out of control because you will have experienced first-hand the consequences of not having control. Something as shocking and tragic as this will act as hard evidence that you don't have any control. You go from not giving a second thought to the unexpected to expecting dangerous things to happen from out of the blue, and so you live in fear of what else might happen.

2 Fear of death, injury or pain

Imagine tripping up on a paving stone and twisting your

ankle: for a while afterwards every time you see a raised paving stone you remember what happened and you feel a bit nervous about it happening again. This is a simple and common example of how a mildly painful experience can make you aware of your body's fragility. So now imagine how you'd feel if you suffered from a serious injury or had a brush with death or if you saw someone else get injured or killed: it makes perfect sense that you would become afraid of something happening again.

When you've had a traumatic experience, it's natural to want to avoid situations where you could be at a similar risk, and this is what happens with PTSD: if you've been mugged or tortured or attacked, you remember the event in so much detail that the fear of it ever happening again becomes extremely intense.

3 Fear of rejection, ridicule or shame

If after a traumatic event you think you're being treated at all differently by people, you will believe that it's because of what happened to you – that because of that event you are less human or even soiled in some way. The fact of the matter is that sometimes people will reject you but sometimes they don't, and more often than not you actually end up rejecting yourself. You want to be the person you were before the incident but if you feel instead that you've been damaged, you see the rejection you feel for yourself mirrored in others.

For example, one of my clients had been raped and during the police investigation procedures she felt as if she had been made to feel dirty. This made her feel rejected.

Her family also didn't know how to react, so, although they didn't reject her as such, as a result of them being awkward and not giving her the love and support she needed, this woman felt that they were rejecting her.

Fear of rejection is very common after a traumatic incident and so is often seen as one of the symptoms of PTSD.

4 Fear of confinement

Flashbacks can strike at any time and in any place, so they can make you feel as if the traumatic event is always ready to pounce on you and trap you. You don't want to go out because that's where the danger is, and you don't want to be at home because even in the safety of your flat or house, you can't escape the flashbacks. You can feel so confined that you believe nowhere is safe: life is literally trapping you and there is no escape or respite.

5 Fear of abandonment or isolation

If you feel rejected or trapped or scared by the world, you'll begin to believe that you are not the person you used to be. You want to run away from yourself because you don't feel like you used to, and because of this you're also convinced that your friends and family will abandon you. You cut yourself off from seeing people because you don't want them to see you in a distressed state and so, ironically, this fear can be self-perpetuating.

6 Fear of something strange or unknown

The events that cause PTSD by their very nature are unusual or unfamiliar. They're not ordinary upsets and common events: they are unusual and traumatic and they happen very rarely. But even though these things – like car accidents or muggings – are not everyday events, because one of them happened to you, you start to believe that the unknown can strike at any time. You generalize this fear of the unusual until you believe that anything that is unknown and unfamiliar is potentially dangerous. You have evidence that this is true because something unexpected and traumatic did happen to you, so you are hyper-aware of your own mortality and the dangers that lurk in the unfamiliar.

As with all fear, the fears related to PTSD should not be ridiculed. They are logical and directly related to the trauma, so even if you can't understand it because you've never had to go through something very traumatic, just think about how you do feel when you get hurt or experience pain. Say, for example, you burn yourself when you're getting something out of the oven: next time you go to take something out of the oven you might feel a bit wary and either take extra care or ask someone else to do it for you.

If you do this after something as insignificant as a small burn, you can see how someone who's been raped might feel afraid of going out on their own; or how someone who was hit by a car is petrified to cross the road. The response of someone who suffers from PTSD is understandable but it is extreme because the situation was extreme.

Case Study

It was an ordinary day and Chris was going through his usual routine: he got off the tube and walked over the railway bridge. But this time he was mugged. His attackers took his mobile phone and his wallet and left him in a serious state: he had been badly kicked and beaten-up and ended up in hospital with a broken nose and cheekbone.

This incident was so traumatic for Chris that it left him suffering from PTSD and triggered all of the six core fears. He was afraid of losing control as he felt he had done at the time. He was scared of the unknown because he'd been attacked when he was going through his regular commute – a routine that was usually familiar. He was worried that if he could be attacked on his way home, anything could happen at any time: in Chris's mind, if you couldn't trust what you knew, how could you trust anything else? He was scared of dying because when he was being attacked, the thought kept going through his mind that he might end up dead. He was afraid of being hurt because he now knew from his injuries what it was like to feel serious pain. He also felt trapped because he couldn't get away from his attackers *and* he was confined by the tube bridge, which was built up on both sides. Chris also felt rejected by the people who were passing by while he was being mugged. We can look at this reaction from a psychological perspective and explain it through what's known as the Bystander Effect – that people don't help because they are afraid of being hurt and mugged themselves – but Chris wasn't aware at the time that some of these people did actually call the police when they were out of sight: as far as Chris was concerned, these people rejected him. He also felt that he'd abandoned himself because he didn't think he'd fought back enough and that life had abandoned him and let him down by letting this happen at all. With the effect of all six of the core fears, Chris felt a massive sense of loss: loss of his security and loss of his sense of self.

Chris suffered from severe flashbacks and during these he relived the whole attack. He remembered falling to the ground and seeing the pavement come towards him; he heard the tube trains passing by and his attackers shouting; he felt afraid that he was going to die; he could feel the pain of being hit and kicked; and he relived the fear and shame of having his belongings taken from him. Chris felt as if his attackers had won. He felt defeated by them, defeated by the situation, and now PTSD was defeating him. Chris went from being a strong man to someone who felt weak, vulnerable and completely out of control. He was totally overwhelmed by his loss of identity and as a result he couldn't function properly on any level: he stopped going to work, stopped going out and didn't want to see anybody at all.

If you suffer from PTSD it's always important to remember that you have been through a lot so it's not surprising that you struggle to cope. We're not talking about one bad day or a negative experience; we're talking about incidents of intense trauma. But if you look at the six core fears of this condition, chances are you have been through them already. Although they may still have a grip on you, you're still here: you have survived. I want you to see how much you are able to deal with – how strong you are – so that when we come to the recovery process you will realize that you are more than able to face your fear.

CAN YOU RECOVER FROM PTSD?

People who are suffering from PTSD tend to focus on what they see as their defeat but I want to make it very clear that anyone who has been through a horrific incident and come out the other side should feel empowered. If you are reading this book because you have had a traumatic experience, whether you are already in therapy or whether you have bought this book to overcome your fear, please take a moment to acknowledge your courage. You are taking steps to deal with your condition and I want you to feel good about that.

PTSD is a complicated syndrome but it is eminently treatable. No matter how much you might feel as if it will never go away, it can and it will. You have to remember that you have survived; you may have been overwhelmed but ultimately that trauma did not defeat you: you're still alive and, no matter how weak you feel, you have to focus on the fact that you are still here.

The recovery process I'm going to take you through will help you put the traumatic incident into perspective. This doesn't mean belittling your experience – because events like rape, mugging, attack or torture are among the most terrifying things in the world: it means putting it in its rightful place.

Ω *How to Treat Post Traumatic Stress Disorder*

We can't make the actual event any less significant but we can make it clear that even though it happened once, or even repeatedly, it is not relentless. What you went through is no longer a threat and you don't have to be afraid any more.

The underlying treatment for PTSD is cognitive behavioural therapy (CBT). CBT focuses on how our thinking causes us to feel and act the way we do. So in the case of PTSD, if we are experiencing unwanted feelings and behaviours – such as flashbacks and panic attacks – it is important to identify what thoughts are causing these and learn how to replace these with more helpful supportive thoughts. It's also common to use other therapies alongside CBT.

I'll explain the recovery process to you in terms of how I treated Chris so that whether you want to help yourself or someone else, you will be able to see very clearly what has to be done and why.

Although you may never meet me, for the treatments in this book to work you need to trust me. I can never know exactly what you're feeling but I am totally sympathetic to your pain and fear. I have experience working with PTSD sufferers – from those who've suffered serious car accidents to victims of organized abuse – and so I know that the recovery process can work. So I will at times be firm with you. I have to be firm and you have to be firm with yourself in order to successfully exorcize your haunting memories; so please have faith in the process and have faith in me.

I Reassure yourself

PTSD attacks you in two ways: you feel as if you're under siege from the outside world because you believe you're constantly in danger, and you also feel under siege from your own internal psychological world because you feel as if you've lost control of your senses. But you mustn't beat yourself up about this: what you're feeling is completely rational. Because of the danger you have had to live through, it's understandable that you're preoccupied with being safe, but I will help you realize that there are other ways in which you can feel safe.

Because PTSD is caused by the fact that the traumatic event is unprocessed, it's essential that the treatment makes it clear that you *can* process the event while feeling safe and in control. This doesn't mean forgetting it; it means putting it where it belongs – in the past. By reminding yourself all the time, you are only bullying and torturing yourself with the memory, and rather than serve to protect you, these constant reminders have the opposite effect. What the treatment process does is show you that you can learn to remind yourself only when you really are at risk.

Case Study

I started off the reassurance process with Chris by making sure that he completely trusted me. He needed to believe that he could safely talk about the event without being judged: he had tortured himself enough and it was time for him to feel supported and cared for.

I did an in-depth assessment of the event and of his flashbacks and we also talked about how he currently felt. Chris told me that he felt trapped by the world because he was afraid of what might happen to him if he went out of his flat, so this became a form of agoraphobia. He also told me how he felt as if his identity was completely different to what it was before the attack.

By talking to someone impartial and learning that his flashbacks were messages from his unconscious to help him deal with the event, Chris started to feel safe. He had taken the first step towards rationalizing his experience and began to see that he could put the event behind him.

2 Organize your thoughts

When you organize and structure your thoughts you will realize that you can control your flashbacks and you don't need to be afraid of them. In order to do this you have to relive the event. This may sound harsh but you are already reliving your trauma every day. The difference is that if you have flashbacks, you are reliving the trauma in a random and uncontrolled way; in therapy we do this in an organized and controlled way, so it's more gentle and easier to cope with.

When you are ready to talk, just relay the *facts*. Don't talk about feelings – only discuss what actually happened. By doing this you agree the story and produce a narrative of what happened. It is only at this point that you moved from the narrative to your thoughts to your emotions.

You can then start to move into the deeper layers of how the event affected you. You can talk about what you *thought* at the time and what you've thought subsequently. Then you move on to the *emotions* you felt then and the emotions you feel now.

This process teaches you how to have cognitive control over how you feel and is based on the principles of Crisis Incident Stress Management (CISM) (Ref: Mitchell, 1983). This is a way of organizing your thoughts about an event and involves discussing both how you felt at the time and how it makes you feel now, deciding what you need to change and then actually letting go of the incident. CISM is widely used to treat the survivors of group traumas, for example, train accidents, plane crashes, natural disasters and acts of terrorism.

With Crisis Incident Stress Management you have to make sure that, whether it's one person or several people who are being treated, everyone taking part had the same exposure to the critical incident and that it is now over for all of them. So if someone was being stalked, you must wait until the stalker has been dealt with and is out of their life. If it was an act of terrorism where people were injured, you can only start CISM once people know the outcomes of any medical investigation, for example, whether they will walk again. The incident has to have been resolved and there must be no more repercussions.

This process, which is also called Narrative Therapy (Ref: White and Epston, 1990), is essential because many people feel as if they're not being listened to. One particularly difficult case I worked on was with a victim of politically sanctioned torture. It was difficult at first for him to get his story down but we had to make sure that he felt his voice was heard. By telling his story, rather than feel ignored, this client felt as if someone cared. In our society, people deal with politically sanctioned torture by not talking about it: in a similar way to the way in which many people react to rape, it's often believed that the best thing to do is silence it. Nobody wants to talk about it because it's difficult and it's extremely painful – but to recover, you have to talk. You have to tell your story.

Case Study

I started by asking Chris to give me a very factual account of his mugging, almost as if he was reporting on it. He wrote down his story and this helped him realize that he didn't need to carry the experience around with him. It could continue to exist on paper, so we weren't trying to belittle or ignore it – just put it in a place where it could be useful rather than traumatic.

Then Chris told me what thoughts went through his head as he was being attacked: *Will I die? Why doesn't someone help? Why is this happening?* He also told me about the punishing thoughts he had when he had flashbacks. *Why didn't I fight back more? Why did I have so much cash on me? Why didn't I go a different way?*

Then we moved on to discuss how Chris felt then and

now. At the time, he felt helpless, scared, in pain and vulnerable. After the event he felt ashamed, guilty and furious that anyone could do that to him.

By getting Chris to interact with his intrusive thoughts, I enabled him to organize them and so get cognitive dominance over them. They no longer controlled him, because he could structure them as he wanted to: he was the one in control.

3 Release and validate your feelings

If you suffer from PTSD you will feel many distressing and confusing emotions such as pain, fear, shame, anger and sadness, and you may also suffer from panic attacks. These feelings won't just surface when you get flashbacks, and for some people the emotions are always in the background of their mind; so because of the number, frequency and severity of these emotions it's important that you deal with them in the right way.

With my client who had been tortured, while he felt validated by getting his story down on paper, it was extremely hard for him to let out his feelings. If we look at what he went through, this is completely logical. Just imagine for one moment how it must feel to be tortured but to never cry or shout or voice your pain. Throughout his torture this man had stayed completely silent, so when I told him that it was OK to voice his feelings he was petrified – but he needed to see that it was rational for him to be distressed and furious. He needed to kick walls and yell and let his emotions have a voice and I had to let him do this for as long as he needed. He deserved to feel that way and he needed to acknowledge that.

By expressing and validating your emotions you are accepting that it is rational and healthy for you to feel the way you do. You are also acknowledging that it's time you allowed your emotions to come out, and the best way to do this is to voice them in a controlled, safe environment.

Case Study

Even if something like this has never happened to you, it's probably very clear to you that Chris deserves sympathy – Chris, however, couldn't see this for himself. He never accepted other people's sympathy and he was extremely hard on himself. Chris felt angry with himself: angry that he hadn't fought back enough, angry that he'd been carrying an expensive mobile phone, and angry that he'd walked the route that he had.

It's very common for people who've been victimized by a traumatic event to give themselves a hard time, because not only do they have to deal with the PTSD, they also have to deal with being victims. Nobody likes the thought of being a victim – but Chris needed to see that the attack wasn't his fault and that it had been very serious and brutal. He wasn't being pathetic, he hadn't done anything wrong – he'd just been unlucky. By condemning his anger and giving himself a hard time for being what he saw as weak, Chris was prolonging his agony. So when he felt safe and strong he let out his feelings and it was critical that he shouted and yelled and cried. He was able to do this because he had learned that these were perfectly rational responses to such a harrowing experience. He had been beaten up and his belongings had been taken from him, so it was OK to be emotional about it.

4 Retain useful information

As I have already said, as much as it may feel as if their only intention is to torture you, flashbacks are the brain's way of reminding you that you have to process the event in order to recover from it. You are unconsciously holding on to the memory, not because you want to, but because the thought of dealing with it is too overwhelming. You don't think you'll be able to cope and don't even know where to start, but your brain is reminding you of the event because there is something within that memory that you have to pay attention to.

So to release and process the event, you have to ask yourself, *What do I need to hold on to from this event?* For example, if you were mugged, you may decide that you could minimize the chance of that happening by walking only on well-lit streets and not having your iPod on view. If you were attacked, you might decide to take self-defence classes.

One thing I want to make very clear is that when you start this process, you have to be careful not to apportion any blame to yourself: you were not a victim because you didn't do these things before. It was not your fault and you didn't deserve what happened to you. What you can do in the future, though, is minimize the risk of that happening again.

Case Study

When Chris thought about how he could feel safer in the future, he decided that he would keep his phone out of sight when he was walking on the street. He also decided that it would help if he walked confidently, slightly faster and with a sense of purpose. Finally he said that if he were ever to be attacked again, he would ask anyone who was passing by to help him. He now knew why the passers-by had carried on walking and that if he'd asked them they would have been more likely to help him. He also learned and accepted that there was no way he could have known this at the time.

Once you've retained any useful information, you can make the decision to let go. That past is over and you can choose to feel safe again. If you do have panic attacks or flashbacks, which you may, you can say, *Thank you for reminding me of what happened but I don't need to hold on to this memory any more* – and then you will be ready to process.

Before we move on to processing, I want to remind you that at every stage in this recovery treatment you must remind yourself that it was not your fault. If you are helping and supporting someone else through their recovery, it is up to you to keep telling them that what happened to them was not because of anything they did. The unexpected can happen to anyone.

5 Process the event

The processing of the traumatic event can be helped using Eye Movement, Desensitization and Reprocessing (EMDR). EMDR was developed by Dr Francine Shapiro, a psychologist at The Mental Research Institute at Palo Alto, California. She realized when she was working with Vietnam War veterans that when they were remembering what happened to them their eyes moved more quickly; and that once their eyes began to move very quickly, they actually began to feel less traumatized. This theory is based on the premise that rapid eye movement helps you to process your thoughts.

This is what happens to us during REM, or dream, sleep. One of the functions of dreaming is to integrate incomplete or unfinished experiences that have either happened in the day or at another time in the past: these are things we didn't fully assimilate or let go of when they occurred. REM sleep finishes this process for us when we're asleep and unconscious of it. We can use this natural way of coping in a therapeutic sense because EMDR allows us to access and reprocess unfinished business from the traumatic incident.

Another way of processing a traumatic event is through hypnosis. Hypnosis is often misunderstood because many people think it's magical mumbo-jumbo, but it's actually a natural phenomenon. We all experience hypnotic trances every day: when we're watching television, dancing, working on a computer, listening to music, thinking about eating delicious chocolate, thinking about how tired we are, or even while we're cooking our dinner. Hypnosis is just a controlled form of a natural state of relaxation.

The power of hypnosis is that it lets you access your unconscious thoughts and these enable you to let go of the traumatic event. You relive the experience while you're in the hypnotic trance and this lets you see that you are able to remember it while feeling deeply relaxed. You don't have to panic or be afraid or upset – you can remember the trauma in a very different state and therefore see it in a very different light.

Note: If you have been working alone or with a close friend up to now, for this stage I suggest you go to your GP, or a psychologist or a therapist who specializes in Critical Incident Stress Management, EMDR and hypnosis. These can all be quite tough and complicated processes, so it will make a huge difference to have the help of a professional.

Case Study

For Chris the processing of his trauma was mainly done consciously. Chris wrote his story and by doing this realized that he felt terrible after only one brief event, albeit traumatic, of being out of control. He accepted that he didn't need to feel terrible because he had survived it and coped with it really well. Chris also reframed how he saw his PTSD: he accepted that his unconscious mind was trying to protect him through his flashbacks, as they were reminding him that he hadn't resolved everything. By seeing this, Chris no longer resented his flashbacks and started to thank them for flagging an issue he obviously needed to deal with. In addition, Chris underwent a course of hypnosis to help him relax and let go of his trauma.

6 Validate yourself

You need to believe that you can get control again and you do this by taking small steps to get your life back to how it was. Start to do routine things that make you feel safe. This doesn't have to mean doing what you were doing when you experienced the trauma – so if you were raped while you were out jogging at night, you don't have to go running in the evening, or if you were attacked on your way home from the office, you don't have to go back to work yet.

If you are suffering from PTSD you will understand what I mean when I say that you start by doing simple things like making a cup of tea, going to the shops to buy a pint of milk, or going outside for a breath of fresh air in the day. These things that most of us take for granted, and that you used to take for granted, are huge steps towards recovery. By feeling in control, you will realize that you are free to do as you please and you're not imprisoned by your past.

I also want you to praise yourself for every small step and

keep reminding yourself that it was not your fault. Forgive yourself for what happened and create a nourishing dialogue in your mind. The final thing is learning how to relax again. Although you may have been able to relax before the event, intense fear can make us forget how to do it. You can couple this recovery process with the breathing exercises in this book or you may do something else – like start to meditate, have an aromatherapy treatment or take yoga classes.

Case Study

Chris started validating himself by nurturing himself through a process similar to the systematic desensitization of a phobia. He started simply by leaving his flat. First of all he walked to the park at the end of his road; then he walked around the park. He praised himself and built up his confidence. He then progressed to crossing tube bridges in daylight and increased every trip out by half a mile until he could cross the same tube bridge where he'd been mugged. He started to feel in control again and so could resume his life as it was. He could see that he was still a strong man and felt that he got his old identity back.

Because mugging is an adult form of bullying, it was critical that Chris stopped bullying himself. He needed to show himself care and acceptance; so he also started to have a positive internal dialogue that focused on forgiving himself. He said to himself:

I know I've been blaming myself but it's not my fault. I don't deserve this. I've lived for 31 years and this has only happened to me once so I am safe most of the time. I don't have to think about this all the time – I can move on. There is a chance of it happening again but I don't have to focus on it because there's a greater chance that it won't happen again. I deserve to move on. I deserve to recover. I deserve to live my life happily.

7 Turn the negative into a positive

At this point it's important to take something positive away from this situation. You will have experienced being as far out of control as you'll ever be and you will also have come to realize the fragility of life, so this is the time to do something that you have always wanted to do. It could be climbing Everest, losing weight, learning to sing, getting married or changing jobs. You've had an experience that has shown you how delicate life can be and so why wait another minute? Why put things off? Do it now! Prove that you are recovered and more in control than you've ever been before: that's when you'll know that you've really beaten PTSD. You have not been defeated. You have won.

Case Study

Chris had always wanted to run a marathon but he never thought he could fit in the training: there was always something better to do. At the end of our session, Chris said that he realized he wasn't prepared to put this off any more. He applied for a charity place in the New York marathon and threw himself into his training schedule.

TAKE-HOME TIPS

Before you get professional help, you can start to take some small steps. These are things you can do on your own right now.

1. No matter what the traumatic incident, say to yourself, *It was not my fault.* If you were raped, it doesn't matter what you were wearing or doing. If you were tortured, it doesn't matter what your political beliefs are. If you were mugged, it was not your fault that you walked that way home or that you were carrying an expensive laptop. The punishment does not fit the crime: it was not your fault.

2. Write out the story of your trauma. If this feels overwhelming, break it into small chunks or just do it for a few minutes.

3. Acknowledge your feelings and tell yourself it's OK to have them. Voice feelings and let them out

These may seem like insurmountable steps, but trust me: they will help you a huge amount with your therapy process. Decide to take these small steps towards being free of your fear and don't let your fear rule you any longer.

ONE FINAL THOUGHT ...

If you are suffering from PTSD, to live the life you deserve to have, you need to treat it. You have to organize your thoughts, acknowledge your feelings and start processing what happened to you. If you don't, the traumatic incident will continue to keep you under siege and the stress will continue to overwhelm you and take over your identity. So no matter how hard it may seem now, I want you to realize that it is possible to treat PTSD and to overcome it completely.

AND FINALLY ...

Hopefully, this book has cleared up any myths you may have had about fear and shown you that, as strange as it may sound, you don't have to be afraid of it! It's OK to be scared. Whether it be for minutes, hours, weeks, months or even years, everybody experiences fear at some point in their life; so you don't have to give yourself a hard time.

Fear is a human emotion and when you experience it, it's because life has thrown something traumatic in your path. This doesn't mean that you're weak or fragile or inferior: it means you've had a lot to deal with and you did so in the way you thought best. But once fear has served its purpose you can let go: it does not have to define you.

By now you will be aware that to break free of your fear, you need to be tough on it. This doesn't mean being angry that it ever existed: it means acknowledging that the emotion was useful to you in the past but now you're ready to move on. While it may have been helpful to you, fear is now an unwelcome guest in your life and you don't need it any more.

As well as being tough on the fear, you need to be gentle with yourself. Being self-critical will only serve to maintain your fear and make it harder to break free. You have suffered enough – so now is the time to be kind.

If anything you've read in this book has resonated with you, please use the information here to start freeing yourself from your fear. If you feel you need or want help, you can visit your GP, speak to a close friend or talk to one of the professional bodies listed below. There is no shame or weakness in asking for help and I hope that this book has taken away the stigma in seeking support.

When I set out to write this book, I wanted to give you all the tools to overcome your fear. So I hope that you now understand fear; that you feel comfortable accessing the relevant support; and, most importantly, that you are able to give yourself the support, belief and motivation to overcome it.

Have hope that you can live a life free of fear.

Dr Lucy Atcheson

Support Bodies

British Psychological Society: www.bps.org.uk
The Samaritans: www.samartians.org.uk, 08457 909090
National Phobics Society: www.phobics-society.org.uk, 0870 122 2325

Post Traumatic Stress Disorder as defined in the Diagnostic and Statistical Manual of Mental Disorders 4th edition (DSM-IV) published by The American Psychiatric Association

To be diagnosed as having PTSD, the following conditions have to be present:

A) Person has been exposed to a traumatic event in which both the following were present:

i) person experienced, witnessed or was confronted with an event or events that involved actual or threatened death or serious injury or a threat to the physical integrity of self or others, and;

ii) person's response involved intense fear, helplessness or horror. Note: in children this may be expressed instead by disorganized or agitated behaviour.

B) The traumatic event is persistently re-experienced in one or more of the following ways:

i) Recurrent and intrusive distressing recollections of the event including images, thoughts or perceptions. Note: in young children repetitive play may occur in which themes or aspects of the trauma are expressed.

ii) Recurrent distressing dreams of the event. Note: in children they may be frightening dreams without recognizable content.

iii) Feelings of the traumatic event re-occurring. This includes a sense of reliving the experience, illusions, hallucinations and disassociative flashback episodes including those that occur on awakening or when intoxicated. Note: in young children former specific re-enactment may reoccur.

iv) Intense psychological distress at exposure to internal or external cues that symbolize or resemble an aspect of the traumatic event.

v) Physiological reactivity to exposure of internal or external cues that symbolize or resemble an aspect of the traumatic event.

C) Persistent avoidance of stimuli associated with the trauma and numbing of general responsiveness not present before the trauma as indicated by three or more of the following:

1. Efforts to avoid thoughts, feelings or conversations associated with the trauma

2. Efforts to avoid activities, places or people that arouse recollections of the trauma

3. Inability to recall an important aspect of the trauma

4. Markedly diminished interest or participation in significant activities
5. Feeling of detachment or estrangement from others
6. Restricted feelings of affect. Unable to have loving feelings
7. Sense of a foreshortened future and impending feelings of doom. The person might not expect to have a career, marriage, children or a normal lifespan.

D) Persistent symptoms of increased arousal not present before the trauma as indicated by two or more of the following:

1. Difficulty falling or staying asleep
2. Irritability or outbursts of anger
3. Difficulty concentrating
4. Hyper-vigilance
5. Exaggerated startle response.

E) Duration of disturbance from criteria B), C) and D) is more than one month.

F) The disturbance causes clinically significant stress or impairment in social, occupational or other important areas of functioning.

Note: PTSD is acute if the duration of symptoms is less than three months and chronic if the symptoms last for more than three months. Delayed onset can also occur if the symptoms begin at least six months after the stressful event.

REFERENCES

Chapter 7

These are taken from McKay, M., Davis, M. and Fanning, P., *Messages: The Communication Skills Book* (Oakland, CA: New Harbinger Publications, 1983)

Chapters 8 and 12

Bourne, Edmund J., PhD, *Anxiety and Phobia Workbook* (3rd edn; Oakland, CA: New Harbinger Publications, 2000)

Chapter 10

Bourne, E. J., *Overcoming Specific Phobias: A hierarchy and exposure-based protocol for the treatment of all specific phobias (client manual)* (Oakland, CA: New Harbinger Publications, 1998)

Chapter 11

Rothbaum, B. O., Hodges, L. F., Kooper, R., Opdyke, D., Williford, J. and North, M. M. (1995) Virtual reality graded exposure in the treatment of acrophobia: a case report. *Behavior Therapy*, 26, 547–554

Chapter 12

Mitchell, J. T. (1983) When disaster strikes ... The critical incident stress debriefing. *Journal of Emergency Medical Services,* 13(11), 49–52

White, M. and Epston, D. *Story, Knowledge, and Power* (New York: Norton, 1990)

Titles of Related Interest

Feel Happy Now, by Michael Neill

Everything I've Ever Learned About Change, by Lesley Garner

Dr Lucy Atcheson's Guide to Perfect Relationships, by Lucy Atcheson

You Can Heal Your Life, by Louise L. Hay

Dawn Breslin's Guide to Super Confidence, by Dawn Breslin

NOTES

NOTES

NOTES